love's energy

love's energy

how to stay in love

john hamwee

FRANCES LINCOLN

For Sophie, Polly and Pippa,
with love and admiration

acknowledgments • • •

I couldn't have written this book at all without the wisdom and inspiration of two people. The teachings of Ram Dass provided the basic orientation of the book as well as many of its key ideas. Dr Fritz Smith taught me most of what I know about energy and he formulated many of the basic concepts I have used. I am very grateful to them. Where I have taken specific ideas and quotations from them and others, I have acknowledged the source in the notes at the end.

Felicity Candogan, Kate Cave, Jake Chapman, Myra Connell, Scilla Elworthy and Cathy Fischgrund all read the first draft and their comments and criticisms were invaluable. If any tedious prose or confused ideas remain, it is in spite of their best efforts. A great deal of what I know about relationships I owe to life and discussions with Scilla Elworthy: I am glad to be able to acknowledge my debt to her. Rosalind Armson and Peter Roberts skilfully explained some basic physics. Fred and Morwenna Curry provided a beautiful place where I could write. Most of all I want to thank Dorsett Edmunds for showing me, by her example, how the theory works in practice.

This book, like so many others, is a tribute to Frances Lincoln's unique talents as a publisher.

contents • • •

since feeling is first
who pays any attention
to the syntax of things
will never wholly kiss you;

e.e. cummings

The basic idea of this book is that it is fascinating and helpful to look at relationships as exchanges and interactions of energy between two people.

The idea can be applied to all kinds of relationships, but I have chosen to focus just on intimate relationships – by which I mean relationships in which romantic love plays a part and the two people concerned share their lives in some way. That covers a wide spectrum; it includes couples who live together, whether or not they are married, and couples who live apart if they feel committed to each other. It also includes couples who keep separating and coming together again at irregular and unpredictable intervals, providing they both feel some kind of deep connection between their two lives. In all these cases the duration of the relationship is irrelevant, as is the gender of the two people. But it isn't about parent and child, sibling or other family relationships, nor about friendships, brief casual affairs or work relationships. The book will be more vivid if you are in an intimate relationship at the time of reading, but it will still be useful if you want to understand what happened in a previous relationship or want to prepare yourself for a new one in the future.

This is not a 'how to do it' book. It doesn't have any exercises you should or must do to improve your relationship; nor does it promise that after reading it your problems will be solved. It does not contain a twelve-step programme to marital bliss. What is does offer is a different perspective on your intimate relationships; that may sound rather theoretical but it is actually immensely practical. Every intimate relationship which doesn't achieve its full potential, still more every relationship which becomes lifeless or unhappy, has ended up that way because the two people came up against some issues which they couldn't resolve. The way they were thinking about the relationship, their attitudes, beliefs and assumptions, didn't enable them to deal with those issues while preserving or enhancing the love between them. What they needed above all was a new perspective; one which could show them things in a new light and suggest new ways of relating to each other. If any couple has that, then they are out of the woods – if they choose to be – and they have an opportunity to enhance the love between them.

There are plenty of other useful perspectives on relationships, and in some cases there are clear and interesting parallels between what I have to say and those explanations of what happens in relationships. However, I don't refer to them in this book, partly because I don't have professional knowledge of them, and partly because I wanted to concentrate on what is, for most people, a novel and provocative idea.

The material in this book comes from two sources. One is what I have learned about how energy works in the human body, and how it interacts with the energy of another body. This is, in my opinion, part of the basic knowledge we all need to make the most of our lives, like knowing how to read and write. The other source is my reflections on some successes and many more failures in my own intimate relationships. Acutely aware of these failures, I often felt like a charlatan writing the book at all. Then I remembered the saying, 'We teach best what we most need to learn.' I think it's true. It means that the clearer you find the book, the more you will realize that you and I are in the same boat; we've all struggled to make sense of what happens in our intimate relationships and to get closer to the kind of love we all seek.

Finally, a word about the use of 'he' and 'she' in the book. It is tedious to keep on reading sentences like 'One partner gets upset so he or she starts to talk to his or her partner about it.' So I have sometimes used 'he' alone and sometimes 'she' alone; in each case what I mean is exactly the same as if I had used the other pronoun. Similarly, when talking of two partners I have referred to one as 'he' and the other as 'she'. What I have to say applies equally to same-sex relationships; I merely wanted to avoid the confusion of a sentence like 'He gets angry, and he reacts' when, by the second 'he', I mean the partner of the one who is getting angry. In short, by my use of personal pronouns I don't intend any statement or comment about gender.

energy and relationships

Experiencing the present with the whole of my body instead of with the pinpoint of my intellect led to all sorts of new knowledge and new contentment. I began to guess what it might mean to live from the heart instead of the head, and I began to feel movements of the heart which told me more surely what I wanted than any making of lists.

Marion Milner, *A Life of One's Own*[1]

We have all had experiences in relationships which are puzzling. Most obviously, there is no knowing when you will fall in love or why. A woman I know was sitting at her kitchen table chopping vegetables. Looking up and out of the window, she saw a man she didn't know walking by outside. In the few seconds in which he was in view she said to herself, with utter certainty, 'I'm going to marry him.' She did, and they are still together, fifteen years later. What on earth happened in those few seconds? How did she know? On the other hand, two people can be friends for years and suddenly, for no apparent reason, one or both of them falls in love with the other. If you've seen the film *Shadowlands* you'll know that this happened in the most dramatic way to C.S. Lewis. He married purely for convenience, so that his American friend would have the right to live in England. At the time of the wedding he made it quite clear that he was just doing her a favour, and there was to be no other obligation on his part. Quite some time later he had the unusual experience, at least in this culture, of discovering that he had fallen in love with the woman who was already his wife. From then on he was devoted to her.

Some experiences are both hard to understand and hard to know how to deal with. For example, you may have found yourself engaged in a curious sort of dance with a partner; it goes like this. You feel full of enthusiasm for him, can't help thinking of things you can do to help him, and have lots of ideas for holidays together. Somehow, he doesn't quite respond with the same energy and gradually your enthusiasm wanes. There is no particular problem, but more and more you find yourself getting on with your own life and not planning things to do with or for him. After a while, when nothing much seems to be happening in the relationship, you begin to notice that he is making all the approaches to you, is starting to initiate plans and projects for the two of you to do together. Whereas before you would have been absolutely delighted with this, and would have wanted nothing more than to join in with a will, now, to your surprise, you find it leaves you rather cold. You say all the right things, and agree that it would be nice to go away in the spring or take in some concerts, but you can feel that you're being a bit formal and polite; your heart isn't really in it. Sooner or later, he starts to withdraw – after all, his efforts aren't having much effect – and you notice a curious thing. Suddenly, you start to get interested again, start to want to spend more time having fun with him and trying new things. And you reflect, with a rueful shrug, that the two of you never seem to get it together at the same time. Your relationship is a bit like an old-fashioned dance; as one of you advances the other retreats, and the two of you never meet in the middle.

When I was caught in this kind of a dance, I spent a lot of time and ingenuity explaining to myself how I was right to advance when I advanced and how wrong my partner was to fail to respond. I also had a host of good reasons why it was right of me to withdraw when she advanced. Then one day it dawned on me that all my reasoning was total nonsense. We were both participating in the dance, and if one of us was advancing the other had to retreat. It didn't matter who was advancing at any one time, or why; nor did it matter who was retreating or why. We were simply collaborating, and, what's more, doing it most precisely. But even when I realized that, I didn't quite know how or why we'd got into the dance, nor how we could get out of it.

Before I start to explain what might be going on here, I want to take one last example of a puzzling thing that happens between couples. It is a pretty common experience, I think, and a very unsettling one. The two of you have had a wonderful time together, you feel very close and warm – indeed you have been especially intimate. You each feel full of love and gratitude towards the other, and are basking in it. You vaguely expect that this heightened feeling will fade away over time, but what happens instead comes as a shock. Suddenly, without warning, you fall from heaven to hell. The last thing you knew were affectionate and tender feelings for each other and now you are both impatient, irritated, or even engaged in a full-blown row. Neither of you wanted that to happen, you both wanted the good feelings to last, and neither of you knows quite how it happened; but there you are looking at each other with hard eyes, painfully aware of the gulf that has just opened up between you.

You might dig back into what was said or done which seemed to trigger this change, but whatever it was doesn't seem important enough, fundamental enough, to have had such a dramatic effect. Something else happened, behind or beyond the words or the actions. What was it? Why did it happen then? And what could you do to prevent it happening again?

This book answers questions like these. It does so by giving you a way of looking at intimate relationships which can explain a good deal of what happens in them and which can help you make the most of them. Sometimes it will suggest how to enhance what is good and what can increase the love and intimacy between you, and sometimes it will explain why you are having a hard time and how you can get through it without harming the relationship or each other. Quite often, as you will see, there needn't be that much difference between them – that is, both the good times and the hard times can generate deeper love and intimacy.

The key idea of the book is that when two people are in an intimate relationship each of their energies is profoundly affected by that relationship. And because a good deal is known about how energy behaves in human beings, it is possible to make reliable generalizations about what the effect will be and how to make the best use of it to help the relationship to flourish.

It's a bit like sailing. If you're in a small boat and you don't know about the winds and the tides, you get blown around all over the place and it is all incredibly frustrating and exhausting. Once you understand the winds and tides, and know how they will affect the boat, you can use their energies to get where you want to go – and you can enjoy the ride. Well, being in a relationship is a bit like being in a small boat; best to know what the energies are doing.

energy

When I talk about energy I don't mean something mysterious or ethereal. I mean something as obvious and everyday as the feeling you have when it's a lovely sunny morning and you're away on holiday in the mountains or by the sea and you can't wait to get out there. Or the lazy, 'can't be bothered' feeling you might have on a cold dreary Sunday afternoon in winter. Or the weariness that comes over you when you have to do some task you hate, like cleaning the gutters or doing your accounts. These are different states of energy. And, as we all know perfectly well, our energy can shift in a moment from one state to another. You get home tired from work, wanting only to slump in a chair and watch TV, and the person you've recently fallen in love with calls up and asks you over for supper; within moments you're in the shower and singing. It can happen the other way too. Feeling well and happy, you get unexpected bad news: the shock of it stops you in your tracks, and leaves you feeling stunned and feeble.

I'm sure you have noticed that other people affect the state of your energy. With one person you might feel small and inadequate, somewhat crushed. It may be partly because of what that person says to you and how you receive what is said. But the words, and your reaction to them, come from something else, from some underlying dynamic or interaction between the two of you which precedes and is expressed by the words. By contrast, in the company of someone else you feel enlivened; funnier, cleverer than usual, more who you want to be. It is normal and reasonable to say that with the first person your energy is drained and depleted, and that with the second it is enhanced and boosted.

In the East, for thousands of years, people have paid very close attention to these common sensations and experiences. They monitored carefully how and when they arise, what they feel like and how they change. They noticed in particular how they are affected by physiological processes such as breath, diet and exercise. They discovered patterns and regularities in the movements of energy, and through a mixture of observation, inference, and trial and error, assembled a coherent body of knowledge about it. The outcome of all this forms the basis for many different kinds of practice, including Yoga and Tai Chi, Acupuncture and Shiatsu. What is relevant here is the general notion that each of us has both a physical body and an energy body. The physical body is the bones, muscles, organs and so on, enclosed in a clear boundary of skin. The energy body is the overall shape and nature of a person's energy. It is a composite of many different flows, rhythms and tensions, a bit like the sound of a symphony played by lots of different instruments. Although most people don't see it or feel it, the energy body is usually a bit bigger than the physical body and roughly the same shape. That's a bizarre sentence! If most of us don't see it or feel it, how can I assert that it is pretty much the same size and shape as the physical body?

One way of knowing that something exists is to take the word of someone you trust. Another is to notice something, and then to find out if others have noticed the same thing. Both of these happened to me. I met Dr Fritz Smith, an unassuming man who took the existence of the energy body as much for granted as the chair he sat on or the air he breathed, who could talk about it convincingly and eloquently, and who had impressive clinical results working with it. I trusted him and his work. Much later I actually felt another person's energy body, and I described it to others who had more experience than me and they confirmed that this was what they felt too. That seemed to me to be reliable knowledge. And, after repeating this procedure for a number of years, like Dr Smith I have become convinced.

In this culture, for some reason, we have enormous difficulty in thinking about movement and flow – we prefer to think of objects. Hence the impossible questions 'Where does your fist go when you unclench your hand?' and 'What happens to your lap when you stand up?'[2] They are impossible questions because we pretend that 'fist' and 'lap' are objects. The words themselves are nouns, but what they describe isn't an object at all, it is a movement. We even have to say 'It is raining' when there isn't an 'it'. The same bias leads us to think of the physical body as a thing, when it is at least as realistic to regard it as a process. Body cells are constantly dying and new ones taking their place; the stomach lining is completely replaced about every seven days; bones take longer but are also in a state of permanent renewal. There are well-attested instant cures from terminal illness. Reputedly, Marie Antoinette's hair went grey overnight. The same bias makes it hard to grasp the idea of an energy body because it is the wave rather than the water, the movement not the molecules.

To give you an idea of what an energy body may feel like and how it can change, I want to tell the story of an energy medicine treatment. My client was a small woman in her mid- to late fifties, well and expensively dressed. She had a challenging look in her eyes and quite a commanding air about her. She told me she had had lots of work from a wide variety of therapists – there was an element of challenge in that too. I asked her what she wanted from the session. It transpired that she was a writer, but she was blocked and couldn't write, which was very difficult for her both emotionally and financially. 'Perhaps,' I thought to myself, 'there is some sort of block in her energy body and she can't find the energy to write until it is unblocked.'

When I came to touch her upper back, there it was. Hard to say exactly what – but something held, restricted, contained, locked away, remote. I had the sensation that I was touching an old and distinct pattern in her energy body, that I had in my hands not just the particular block but, somehow, her basic propensity or habit of blocking – of which this writing block was just the latest manifestation. And, using the techniques in which I am trained, I felt it clear. Then, it seemed to me that clearing the block had left that part of her energy body empty, uncertain how to fill up or reassemble itself. So I did some more work and suddenly there it came. Like the tide coming in, or a newly dug well starting to fill, or a piece of machinery long seized up which has been extravagantly oiled – the energy suddenly starting to move in a rhythmic pulse.

Immediately after the session she said she felt taller – a fairly standard response to this kind of work. Then she added, 'It is that, but it's not quite that. I'm on the same level as other people now. I look straight at them, on a level.' As she said it, it was clear from her face that this was crucial to her. I didn't know why, because she didn't explain; nor could I see what it had to do with the issue of a writer's block. But she was reporting what I took to be a change in her energy body, so I could only hope that it would work. Later she sent me a piece she had written in the days after the session, an inspiring account of her daughter's serious illness and recovery.

This is one subjective experience. But there is an increasing volume of scientific research which points to the existence of the energy body. Harold Burr, Professor of Anatomy at Yale Medical School from 1933 to 1956, researched it for three decades and published over ninety papers about it. Another pioneer is Valerie Hunt, a distinguished neurophysiologist.[3] She discovered ways to measure what she calls the energy field of a human body – which is more or less what I mean by the energy body. That is, her instruments can pick up a distinctive area surrounding the body, one which is qualitatively different from an area, say, twenty yards away, and also different from the area surrounding any another body. In one of her many experiments she placed two people in a room, on chairs, back to back. Then she measured changes in their respective energy fields as they sat there. What she found was that in some cases the energy field of one person invaded and took over the energy field of the other – rather as one red pair of socks in the washing machine will turn a white shirt in the same wash into a pink one. In other cases, the two energy fields blended into each other, so that each person's field was altered by contact with the other, and both ended up pretty similar, like two colours mixing. Finally, sometimes the two energy fields bumped up against one another, but, like two billiard balls making contact, neither was changed by the contact.

When I first read about this experiment I was fascinated. I recognized all three of these instances from my own experience, but I had never expected that there would be any scientific validation of them. I thought of a particular relationship I had been in, where my energy body seemed to be invaded and taken over; would it have been possible, I wondered, to make some change so that our two energy bodies became more similar, somehow more equal? Did gender make a difference? Were there other ways of relating, apart from these three? What would happen to their energy bodies if the two people were in love, or furious with each other? In other words, I began to see that in any close relationship, especially an intimate one, each person's energy body would be hugely affected by his or her partner's, and, indeed, that the way each energy body was affected might explain so many of the things I'd always found puzzling about my own relationships.

In the rest of this book, I am going to take the existence of the energy body for granted. If you don't believe in it, or aren't sure, just take it as a hypothesis, as a useful working idea, which you can jettison later if you decide it isn't true. But while you are reading, and reflecting on your own relationships, see if it makes sense of your experiences. It's best to be both sceptical and to have an open mind.

Here is an example of using the energy body as a working idea. Perhaps you can remember a time when you and your partner weren't communicating well; you'd be unusual if you couldn't. Sometimes it is obvious what is going on; one or both partners is angry with the other and they daren't open up the contentious issues for fear of what will happen if they do. Sometimes it is less obvious but more depressing; in her view, for example, he misunderstands whatever she says and takes it the wrong way. So conversations never get anywhere because she spends the whole of her time trying to explain the very first thing she wants to say, and she never gets on to the important part. From his point of view, he's heard what she has to say many times, and he's trying to point out something new about the situation, not just rehash old and stale positions. But she doesn't seem to listen.

When communication breaks down, each person tends to adopt whatever strategy they use when faced by difficulties in life generally. What often happens is that one resolutely denies that there is a problem – 'I'm fine. I don't particularly want to talk anyway. What is there to talk about?'

Meanwhile the other really wants to sort it out, to resolve it through a deep and meaningful conversation about the problem; what one of my children, with dread, refers to as a 'heart to heart'. It's an impasse.

A couple can also collude in creating an impasse. They agree warmly that it would be good to talk, and they both say that they really want to get to the bottom of it and sort it out, but they never manage to find the right time, or they go through the motions of talking while making sure that neither really opens up to the other, or expresses pain, frustration, disappointment, anger – whatever is uncomfortable.

I imagine that all books about relationships have suggestions and advice about how to deal with failures of communication; certainly the ones I have read all discuss it. Basically they suggest different ways in which the partners can talk and listen to each other, and a lot of what they say is worthy and helpful. But what does this problem look like from the perspective of energy, and what does that perspective suggest would be a good way to resolve it?

Take the analogy of radio. If you want to receive a particular radio station you have to tune your radio to pick up its signals. Without getting too technical, each signal has a particular vibration; it is a wave with a specific height and depth and which vibrates a specific number of times each second. It's a sound wave. When you tune the radio you adjust something inside it (you can tell I'm not a scientist) so that it resonates with that particular vibration. This is a good analogy because each person's energy body has a particular vibration too. There's more about this later, but for now all you need to know is that it is unique and individual to that person, that it can change very quickly, and that it can be sensed by another person.

So when communication between a couple breaks down I want to say that neither partner is tuned to the vibrations of the energy body of the other. Actually, I want to go further and suggest that it may be because they aren't tuned in that the communication has broken down. Messages sent from one to the other – whether they are in words, gestures, body language, actions – aren't being received. So they are each going their own merry way, not realizing that they haven't the faintest idea what their partner is trying to tell them or appreciating that their partner hasn't the faintest idea why they are doing what they are doing. I'm exaggerating a bit, but you must have had the experience that someone has heard your words but they haven't understood what you meant by them. However clearly you express yourself there's something else, something which has to be in place, that makes the words into communication. Equally, you've probably had the opposite, and wonderful, experience when you and your partner have understood each other perfectly with a single word or through the slightest momentary glance.

So much for the diagnosis; what's the remedy? It is clearly to get the two energy bodies in tune with each other, so that each can receive the messages being sent by the other. There are lots of ways of tuning into each other; I describe quite a few of them throughout the book. But the simplest and one of the most effective is to spend time together doing something you both really enjoy. I know it sounds awfully feeble and rather naive, but there is a sound physiological basis for it (explained in later chapters) and it works. It doesn't matter what you choose to do together – it can be as active as jogging or digging the garden, as passive as sitting in a room listening to music or doing nothing. It works best if you are alone and you don't talk much; just say what absolutely has to be said about whatever you are doing at the time, nothing about any other issues. I can't predict how long it will take – if the misunderstanding was small it might take ten minutes, if it was part of a serious conflict it might take many hours spread over a week or so. But it is a quick and reliable method for re-establishing communication.

How do you know when you've spent long enough? It'll be obvious. The atmosphere between you will change, you'll be comfortable again in each other's company, you'll start to smile at each other, maybe even laugh at the same things. Simple requests will get an immediate response; one of you, unprompted, will do something for the other which is readily accepted. When some of this, at least, starts to happen, keep going for a while just to be on the safe side. Then, if you need to, you can talk about whatever burning issues were dividing you beforehand. What often happens is that you find you don't need to talk about them any more; they seem less important, less interesting than they were. That's mainly because they were the vehicles through which you each expressed your unhappiness or dissatisfaction or frustration with the relationship: now it is better, you don't need them so badly any more. If you do need to talk you'll find it much easier to reach agreement; you will be communicating again at a level behind and beneath the words.

orientation

This example contains two ideas which challenge conventional assumptions. The first addresses the assumption that making changes in a relationship is an arduous business: the partners will need, at least, to get clear about the problems they have, work to uncover their causes and then deal with them one by one. Behind that assumption is the difficulty, again, of thinking in terms of movement and flow. If you can see a relationship as fluid and volatile, because it is the co-creation of two energy bodies which are themselves fluid and volatile, then you will know that it can change in a moment. If you can look at your relationship from the perspective of energy, then you don't have to make Herculean efforts to try and impose change on an apparently solid and intractable state of affairs. What you do have to do is to notice how energy works between you so you can feed what works well and starve what doesn't.

There is an image which conveys the difference between these two approaches.[4] Imagine that two pieces of wood are joined by a dowel – that is, each piece has had a circular hole drilled in it, the holes are lined up and a small cylinder of wood, the dowel, has been hammered through both, joining them firmly. Now, if that dowel has rotted away, the join won't hold: so how to repair it? One way would be to use a pin or a narrow blade and to scrape out all the rotten wood. That is the equivalent of focusing on what is wrong in a relationship, and making an effort to change it; removing, painstakingly and painfully, all that isn't holding the couple together. The other way is to get a new dowel and simply tap it in. As it goes in it will push out the old dowel. There is no need to excavate the debris. What is old and weakened will simply be replaced by what is new and stronger. Attending to the energy of a relationship should have the effect that gradually, without noticing, almost accidentally, what doesn't work is replaced by what does.

It's really a matter of orientation. I'll never forget reading *Iron John* by Robert Bly, a book about becoming a man.[5] For the first chapter or two, as he set out what had to be done to attain this state, I was really excited; 'Oh yes,' I thought, 'that's what I have to do. Great, I'll start tomorrow.' By chapter five, there were just so many things I had to do, apparently, that the whole thing felt utterly hopeless. I threw the book away, put my feet up on the sofa, opened a beer and watched football on TV (not the kind of man he was getting at).

The other idea which is basic to all that follows is the importance of simply paying attention. At the end of the example about communication, I said that you would know when the energy between the two of you had changed because 'the atmosphere between you will change, you'll be comfortable again in each other's company'. Of course, if you aren't paying attention to these things you won't notice a change. Some people find this easier than others; there are those who seem to have antennae which pick up an atmosphere accurately and instantly. But how easy it is depends mostly on how interested you are. A village blacksmith liked watching period drama on TV because there was so much excellent ironwork to be seen; I've watched period drama too but I've never noticed the ironwork.[6] If you want to know what is going on in your relationship, if you want to take advantage of the opportunities it presents, then you'll need to pay attention to the state of its energy. In order to do that it helps to have some pointers as to where to look and what to look for; there are plenty of pointers in the following chapters.

Taking this idea of attention a step further, I want to suggest that, in relationships, attention works better than intention.[7] Most of the emphasis in this culture is on intention; we are taught to set goals so we know what we're trying to achieve; organizations have to have mission statements, teaching materials need 'aims and objectives', and so on. There isn't much support for the idea that simply paying attention to something makes a difference. There are exceptions; the idea of simply being a witness, observing but not intervening directly in a conflict, is a cornerstone of Quaker mediation and peacekeeping. And practitioners of meditation have long been taught to pay the closest possible attention to their breath, and have discovered that all sorts of physical and mental changes flow from that. The following two authors, the first writing about quantum physics and the second about the spirits of plants – it is hard to imagine two more disparate perspectives – reach the same conclusion.

> From its earliest days quantum theory has implied that something very odd, and of crucial importance, happens when we observe a quantum system. Unobserved quantum phenomena are radically different from observed ones . . . Not only does observation somehow . . . give us a world in the first place, but it turns out that the particular way in which we choose to observe quantum reality partly determines what we shall see.
>
> Danah Zohar, *The Quantum Self* [8]

Now plant spirits:

> . . . energy knows when it is being watched . . . Energy responds to us.
>
> Eliot Cowan, *Plant Spirit Medicine* [9]

It isn't exactly novel to say that the quality of your relationship depends, to a considerable extent, on the amount of attention you give it. But when people say that, they usually mean paying attention to a partner's wishes, needs and expectations. In essence, the rest of this book is about how to pay attention to energy. Sometimes, as when you are just starting a new relationship, it'll be about paying attention to the way in which your two energies are joining so that they can meet easily and harmoniously. Sometimes, as when you're angry with each other, it'll explain how to pay attention in order to manage and contain that explosive energy. Sometimes it'll be about how to pay attention to the way you touch each other so that the sexual contact between you can meet your deepest yearnings. Mostly it'll be about how to pay attention so that the energy of your relationship can enhance and deepen the love between the two of you.

falling in love

One problem with the rational approach to romantic love is that love is treated as a purely interpersonal matter of human dimensions. Mythology and poetry teach us to imagine this kind of love differently . . . Love is divine, and if we don't recognize this fact and treat it with some piety, then clearly we will be its victims.

Thomas Moore, *Soul Mates*[1]

You don't jump in love, you fall in love. It's involuntary. You can't make it happen when you want, you can't make yourself fall in love with someone suitable, and you don't know where you're going to land. It is often heart-breaking and there's usually a lot of fear involved, but it is still irresistible. The core romantic story of Romeo and Juliet is re-enacted every day. It makes no difference if it is inconvenient or upsetting to those you care about or if it involves ditching all sorts of fixed opinions and beliefs, it still happens. It can even happen when you know that the person you've fallen in love with doesn't love you. The reward is that when you fall in love, everything is more intense, more dramatic, more keenly felt. Your senses are heightened – you see more vividly and hear more acutely; every touch is sensual. You feel as if you've come alive. What is this phenomenon? What has changed, and how? And what can we learn from it which can help us to live at something approaching this kind of joyful intensity at other times?

One way of answering these questions is to use the analogy of a radio again. When you fall in love it is as if your energy body is tuned to a different frequency; it picks up a different stream of messages. They certainly aren't the messages of normal life and normal coping. Rather they are messages which inform us of another way of being, of the possibility of living with a more alert awareness of life.

vibration

The energy body has a particular vibration. When a person falls in love, the vibration of the energy body changes. I'll come shortly to how it changes, and what that tells us about love, but I need first to say a bit about vibration.

We know vibration best from music; we recognize the distinctive sounds of a piccolo, an oboe and a double bass. The first of these has the highest vibration and the last the lowest. Machines which measure sound show notes played by a piccolo as short rapid waves and notes from a double bass as long slow waves; the instruments create vibrations of different frequencies. Driving too fast in low gear, to use another image, you can feel the engine revving hard. When you change up a gear the vibration drops and, of course, the engine uses less energy. Like musical instruments and car engines our bodies also have a vibration. By comparison with other animals or organisms, all human bodies have the same vibration; compared with other human bodies, each body has a unique one. As one scientific writer puts it:

> Vibrations underlie virtually every aspect of nature. The vibrations of atoms create sound and heat. Light arises from the vibrations of electrons in an object . . . In the living body, each electron, atom, chemical bond, molecule, cell, tissue, organ (and the body as a whole) has its own vibratory character.
>
> James L. Oschman, *Energy Medicine: The Scientific Basis*[2]

Apart from the science, the term 'vibration' describes a common perception. Some people are quick and, well, energetic; they tend to rush about, walk fast, and their small movements have a sudden jerky quality. Often they have similar mental qualities; they jump from one idea to the next and are easily bored. They tend to eat a lot and stay thin; rather like the high revving engine, they just gobble up energy. At the other end of the scale are those who are slow speaking and slow talking, liking to take time over things, to the point, even, of lethargy. Figure 1 gives a visual representation of these opposites. Of course, these are two caricatures; still, if you think of people

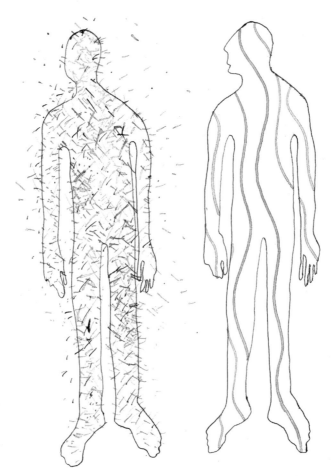

figure 1

you know, I suspect you will be able to call to mind an overall vibration, one which they have most of the time even if, on some occasions, they are revving higher or lower than usual. In fact, when someone really changes his or her vibration, it can be quite alarming. The highest revving person I ever knew – he was in the SAS – sometimes used to walk incredibly slowly. It gave an impression, no doubt carefully cultivated, of immense power and potential. I'm thinking too of the rare occasions when a very fat person moves very fast; you realize with a shock that there is a real crisis afoot.

The vibration of an energy body can be more or less organized. The issue here is whether all the different vibrations of all the different parts of the body are resonating harmoniously together, or whether, like an orchestra where the instruments are not in tune and are all being played to a different rhythm, they are contradictory and chaotic.

In people, a highly organized energy body usually manifests as a kind of clarity. Top athletes have it, at least when they are performing, and so do many mothers with their newborn babies. In fact anyone who is truly at ease with him or herself tends to have it – and it may be that it is because their energy is so coherent that they are at ease. By contrast, the energy bodies of those who are in some period of transition in their lives, like teenagers or those going through a divorce, tend to be disorganized. There are sudden shifts of mood and inconsistent behaviours; there can be times of intense activity alternating with times of lassitude.

In India, it is commonplace for people to touch the feet of a guru. They do this because the guru's energy body is more organized than their own. Some people, perhaps the majority, are unaffected by the touch, but many are profoundly changed. In essence, the highly organized energy of the guru has overridden their more muddled and chaotic energy, in much the same way that creases are ironed out of cloth. Physical and emotional pain, which were held in place like creases in the energy body, are smoothed away. I shall have more to say, later, about the relationship between healing and changes in the energy body.

The vibration of the energy body also gives it its shape. The most obvious aspect of this is sheer size. People who are ill seem to shrink – it isn't the physical body that it shrinking, it is the energy body. All their energy is being taken up in fighting the illness, so there is much less projecting beyond the boundaries of the physical body. People who are successful or famous have an extraordinary kind of magnetism which reaches out and socks you. I met the Queen once. From a distance she looked like an ordinary, though rather well turned-out, elderly woman. But when she got within about six or seven yards the impact hit me; it was like bumping into an invisible cushion. Famous people (except, I imagine, Woody Allen) tend to have large energy bodies.

The energy body is roughly the same shape as the physical body, but there may well be places where the correspondence isn't exact. The energy body of one young woman I worked with was much bigger on the right-hand side of her body than on the left. I gave her an energy treatment which evened them up again, and, much later, she realized why it had happened. She had spent a couple of evenings with a man she'd just met, and to whom she had initially been attracted. In the course of those evenings she had come to dislike him, even to be afraid of him, and had told him she didn't want to see him again. She was glad that she had never told him where she lived. Late one night she answered the doorbell, expecting a close friend who was arriving to stay with her. As she opened the door, there, on her doorstep was the man. It was a dreadful shock. She realized, after the treatment, that as the shock hit her the right-hand side of her body was behind the half-open door, whereas the left-hand side was exposed. As a result, her energy body on that side had contracted. That is not surprising; if you can recall a time when you had a shock you can probably remember that feeling of contraction – you may even remember it affecting a specific part of your body. When I got unexpected bad news I felt as if I'd been punched in the stomach. As a result of physical injury or emotional pain the energy body may be diminished in some areas.

I turn now to the implications of all this.

love as energy

When a person falls in love the energy body changes; it vibrates to a different frequency, it gets bigger and becomes more organized. The feeling of falling in love, and all the remarkable sensations and effects associated with it, can be seen as a result of the combination of these three simultaneous changes in the energy body.

The subjective sensation of the expansion of your energy body is that you feel physically bigger than before, and with that goes a feeling that you are stronger, more important, more valuable. Instinctively, you claim the right to be where you are and who you are. For many people, this is a huge change; feelings of being unimportant, or, as a woman once said to me, 'a waste of space', are very common. These feelings disappear, at least temporarily, as the energy body expands. The reason for this is that as it expands there is an inconsistency between the old habitual feeling of being small and the new experience of being big; an inconsistency which has to be resolved. Sometimes the old feeling will prevail, and the outcome is that the new experience, and the new lover, are both rejected; the mind makes sense of that by reasoning that such a small and insignificant person cannot possibly have been loved, the whole thing was an illusion or a mistake, and thank goodness you realized all that before you made a fool of yourself. Alternatively, accepting the current experience of expansion and self-worth as true, you abandon your inconsistent belief in your smallness. And what feelings of relief and of joy come with that.

This is an example of the way in which falling in love can be so healing. These old beliefs which we lug around, most of them amounting to a lack of self-worth, are limiting and deadening. But getting free of them is no easy matter. There are many methods for doing it – psychotherapy and spiritual practice are two of them which have worked for many people – but they both take a long time and require a good deal of discipline. By contrast, falling in love is like magic. You get an instant release without the effort. At least, that is what happens initially; with this method, the effort comes later.

Your energy body also changes its shape when you fall in love. Physical and emotional wounds can leave it distorted in a variety of ways. I once gave a treatment to a woman who had broken her lower arm about eighteen months before, and still couldn't use her hand properly. The fingers couldn't grasp at all well, she had very little range of movement in her wrist, and, most troublesome of all, the hand only responded slowly, and apparently reluctantly, when she told it what she wanted it to do. X-rays showed that the bone had healed perfectly, and none of the other tests she had could find anything amiss. But when I touched her arm it felt dead and empty and lifeless – good indications that although the physical body had healed the energy body had not. Indeed, it took only one energy treatment to restore full use of her hand.

Emotional wounds affect the energy body too; a common phrase for the feeling of betrayal is to say that it was 'a stab in the back'. I have felt it myself, and it was just like that. Perhaps this is a way of reporting the sensation of a sharp cut in the energy body; I suppose it is felt in the back because you don't know that area of your body – you can't see it – just as you can't see and don't know when you are being betrayed. As with a cut in the physical body, it needs care and time in order to heal. To take one more example, I'm sure you've seen someone put a hand over his or her heart in response to a verbal attack. There is no physical threat, and the gesture is not a protection of the physical body; it is an instinctive protection of the energy body in the area of the heart.

Over time, distortion in the energy body will have an effect on the physical body. Drooping shoulders tell a history of loneliness and being uncared for, and of resignation about these things. That is because it is through the arms that we receive from others and give to them, and with the arms that we nourish ourselves; if these activities have become infrequent, mechanical, loveless, then the energy body around the shoulders will become shrunken and thin, and that will eventually alter the shape of the physical body. The woman whose left and right sides were different, following her shock on opening the door to an unwelcome visitor, is another instance. If she hadn't recovered from that shock, she would have ended up holding her body in some lopsided way.

Love can heal these wounds in the energy body. With some wounds, this will happen simply as the energy body expands; it is easy to imagine that drooping shoulders will pick up as the shrunken energy in and around them fills out through giving and receiving love. With other wounds, a specific change in the energy body may be needed. Imagine a man who in childhood was regularly punished for saying what was unwelcome, and got into the habit of not telling the truth. In later life, this has caused endless problems in his relationships. The outcome of all this is that his energy body is very weak in the area around his throat. If he is lucky enough to find a partner who loves him as he is, and who can cope with hearing what she doesn't particularly want to hear, he will discover that he can tell the truth without incurring catastrophic consequences. Slowly the old pattern of behaviour can be healed. And one outcome will be that the hole in his energy body will fill in. It can be done the other way round too; if he manages to fill in the hole in his energy body, through practices such as Yoga or Chi Gung or by having energy medicine treatments (see appendix one, page 128), the consequence will be that he will find it progressively easier to tell the truth.

There are lots of ways of altering the energy body, and the expansion that occurs when a person falls in love can certainly do it. If this seems like magic, it is only because the mechanism of energy, the way it works, is not generally understood.

The general point is that although we categorize lots of different bits of human beings – the brain is different from muscles – and we categorize lots of different levels too – the movements of the intestines are different from feelings of compassion – the awkward fact still remains that all these are part of one person. Change one part and you cannot help having an effect on the whole. Changes in the energy body can affect emotions, beliefs, attitudes and habits as well as knees and intestines and the senses. Smell, taste, sight, sound and touch are not just mechanical capabilities; without any variation in the mechanisms, there are times when our senses are heightened and times when they are dulled. It isn't some poetic nonsense to say that the world looks a brighter place when you've just fallen in love; it is an accurate description of the consequences of an energetic change. In this sense, being in love is simply restoring to us our true capabilities, the fullness of pleasure we can have from perceiving what is in front of our eyes and under our noses. Perhaps that it why it feels so right to be in love; it returns us to our true state. Although there are other ways of regaining our senses – an evocative phrase – it happens so quickly and effortlessly when we fall in love that we can't help believing that it's the only way to do it.

Perhaps more important, we can't help believing that we can only do it with that one special person. As we shall see, the energy of love suggests that both of these beliefs are wrong.

Being in love organizes the energy body so that all the separate parts are working together harmoniously and consistently. It is very like what happens in a task group in which all the members get on well personally, all are helping and supporting each other, and all have the same commitment to the group's aims. It is a benign circle. The happier each person is at work, the better the group's output; and the better the group's output, the happier each member becomes. A person with a more organized energy body experiences much the same kind of increase in capability, potential and sense of self-worth.

All this is amplified if two people fall in love with each other at about the same time; then both of their energy bodies take on the same vibration and become organized in the same way. As you may know, if two violins both have one string that is tuned to exactly the same pitch, and a violinist plays one of those strings, the same string on the other violin will sound the same note, even if it is at the other end of a room. That is what it is like when the energy bodies of two people have the same vibration and organization. There is a common phrase which captures this kind of mutual resonance; people say 'we are on the same wavelength'. To others, the couple in love seem somehow separate, enclosed, as we say, 'in a world of their own'. To each other, there is the strange experience of recognizing the other as part of oneself; of feeling not two but one. Looking deep into the other's eyes, as lovers are wont to do, each sees him or herself looking back. I'm reminded of the first time a child looks in a mirror, knows who it is and can't stop looking for the sheer fascination of it. Perhaps what is being recognized is a mirror image of the vibration and organization of one's own energy body. And if the couple are sleeping together, that is spending about a third of each day very close to each other, the two energy bodies blend into one another. The normal boundary of the energy body which each of them preserves in ordinary life overlaps and dissolves into the other; it becomes difficult to know where one person's energy body ends and the other's begins. The experience is of being united with each other. It feels so special that couples talk of having found the person they've been looking for all their life, a soul mate; a person who, though obviously different, is also exactly like themselves. No wonder they are surprised into making these kinds of claims.

Some of you may think I am painting a rather rosy romantic picture, exaggerating the power and novelty of these sensations. Of course, it may not have been like that for you; but I would be surprised if there wasn't a change which you could now see as an increase in the vibration, extent or organization of your energy body. I have a particular reason for making this claim. As you have been reading I expect you have had an underlying assumption that what I am doing is translating what we know as falling in love into these categories of change in the energy body. That is, all this stuff is just a matter of putting love into a new and different language. But it might be the other way round. It might be that what we call falling in love is just a short and conventional way of talking about what has happened to our energy bodies. I have particular reason for thinking it might be that way round.

The reason is that all the phenomena and emotions and heightened senses which we all recognize as part and parcel of falling in love can happen in completely different circumstances, and without a partner at all. Mother Teresa, admittedly an extreme example, was asked how she could bear to spend her life picking up destitute people from the gutters of Calcutta, people with terrible afflictions, gaping and infested wounds, rampant disease. She looked rather surprised at the question. She replied, 'I am tending my beloved [by which she meant Christ] in all his distressing disguises.' That's an extraordinary and moving statement of love. I'm sure her attitude is shared by many monks and nuns, whatever religion they profess and whatever the particular work they do. The way they talk about the state they are in – 'tending my beloved' – and the heightened senses which they report are very similar to the experience of secular love. George Herbert, the deeply devout seventeenth-century cleric, wrote a number of poems called 'Love' which address God in language which is charged with sensuality. Those who have met the Dalai Lama report much the same thing; he seems to be in love with everyone he encounters. He regards each person with the same kind of appreciative wonder as a new lover, and few people are unmoved by the experience. It is as if his attitude is, 'Why be selective? Why not be in love with everyone?'

People also fall in love with causes and campaigns to change something they find unjust; if you think this is an exaggeration, consider the revolutionaries who have devoted their lives to a cause and are prepared to die for it. From what I have seen and read about her, it seems that Dian Fossey, who devoted herself to the protection of the mountain gorillas of Central Africa and sacrificed her life in the process, felt love for them. If all these different objects of love create the same, or at least very similar, effects in the lover, then what is the commonality, what is it that is the same irrespective of what is loved? I suggest it is a particular kind of change in the energy body.

This leads to a rather startling conclusion. When you fall in love you aren't really falling in love with some other person. You are falling into a different state of being; into a heightened sense of what it is to be human. We all of us have the potential to be the way we are when we have just fallen in love, and to be it all the time. What feels like a fresh and more alive way of living in the world is, in a sense, our birthright. It is who we really are and what we are really like underneath all the learned behaviour and the social norms and the fitting-in. What with everything else that is going on, and all the things we have to do, we've just forgotten, that's all. There is a common phrase which recognizes this truth. People say, usually as a put-down, 'You're just in love with being in love.' Exactly. Being in love is the state to be in, and we love it.[3]

Most of us can't get there, can't arrive at this state, without some other person to launch us unwittingly into it. Like a boat that takes us to an idyllic island, the loved one is, as it were, our means of transport; we can't get there without him or her. That person stimulated the change in our energy body which takes us to this state. That's why we want to be with the loved one all the time, and that's why we get so fearful and anxious if we think he or she is going to leave us, or think that the love won't last. We can't bear the prospect of going back to how we were before, of losing what we had when we were in this new state.

If you are a confirmed romantic, you'll probably want to throw the book away at this point. But if you misunderstand how the energy of love works, then the danger is that what you do to hold on to it might well have the opposite effect of driving it away; and once again you'll be surprised and disappointed that the relationship didn't work out the way you hoped and dreamed it would. Most of us have done that through our yearning for love.

blame and beyond

This perspective on love makes some sense of the mysterious and horrible process of falling out of love. How can it be that the person who once lit up your life, who was so wonderful that you couldn't bear to live without him or her, can become someone about whom you can see nothing remarkable at all? Leaving aside the rows and resentment which, for obvious reasons, often accompany the end of any relationship, what I am talking about is a particular change; from the other being special to the other being ordinary. When you fall out of love you wonder, 'Was I deluding myself when I thought he was special?' or 'How did she manage to conceal her ordinariness from me for so long?' Because there seems to be such an unbridgeable gap between 'special' and 'ordinary', you naturally ask yourself these kinds of questions. The answers you will come up with won't make much sense because if you ask a meaningless question you get a meaningless answer. The one you loved was both special and ordinary at the same time. To some extent, he seemed special because his energy body was expanded and organized; it gave him a kind of shine or gloss which was delightful. But it didn't change his personality or habits; the ordinariness was there all along. The real reason you saw him as so special is basically because of the change in your own energy body. That coloured everything, and coloured it brighter. It coloured him brightest of all because he was the person who triggered it all off. However, when your energy body contracted back to the way it was before, resumed its old rather disorganized state, everything looked normal again, including him. You may conclude that he has changed, and be pretty angry with him – he's not who he was: what a letdown. Or you may feel guilty, sensing vaguely that you have changed, and concluding that it's all your fault.

There are all sorts of reasons why the energy body contracts and loses its coherence – they are discussed in later chapters. The point for now is that this accounts for the perceived change in the loved one, and it explains at least some of the pain and anger and resentment which come along with what we call falling out of love. It is a kind of eviction from the garden of Eden. If the process of falling out of love is a contraction and disorganization of the energy body, and a shift in its vibration, then it is obvious why people like Mother Teresa and the Dalai Lama don't fall out of love with anyone. Decades of meditation and prayer made their energy bodies what they are, and they can sustain them in the face of indifference, opposition and hostility from others. As no one else got them into that state, no one else can remove them from it either.

In saying this I am not suggesting that we should all give up romantic love and take to prayer. On the contrary; for most of us romantic love, and the development and deepening of it with a partner, is the only way we can gain access to a state of being which enhances life for us and for all around us. What I am proposing is that if we are aware that being in a state of love entails a change in our energy body, then we can learn all sorts of ways of boosting its power and scope, of preserving it through the hard times and rescuing it if it seems to be slipping away. All of these topics are covered later. But perhaps more important than any of that is the change of perspective that comes simply from learning to see love and relationships in this way. There is a lot of blame in most intimate relationships, and it causes a lot of suffering. Some of it is blame of the other, the complaining 'If only you would love me the way you used to.' More of it is blame of oneself, the mortified 'If only I had been more attentive, more interested in her concerns, she would still love me.' And all of it is a distraction and a delusion. None of it helps to create, or recreate, the state we all want to live in, where we can see ourselves and others with the eyes of love.

If, instead, we can see love as energy, then we can lose the habit of blaming. Blame becomes irrelevant. If you are a surfer, you don't blame a wave that crashes on you. Understanding how waves are, you learn to ride them. Those who understand them best ride them with ease and grace and pleasure; they may fall off sometimes, but they don't spend the rest of their lives blaming the wave or blaming themselves for the fall and refusing to surf ever again. If you understand love as a force which rises up, somewhat like a wave, and which can carry you on an exhilarating ride for the rest of your life, you can learn to ride it more easily and more often, and learn not to take yourself too seriously if you fall off every now and then.

touch and intimacy

When something is touched very deeply it reveals itself to us. No talking, no thinking – just breathing and looking.

Thich Nhat Hanh[1]

Heaven knows there's enough written about sex, but there is one absolutely essential aspect of it which is hardly ever mentioned, and which most people know nothing about. It is touch. Sex without touch doesn't really work, and yet we take touch for granted. We reckon that the way we touch someone must be all right – after all, how else could we do it? We probably hardly even register the way our partner touches us; like the way they laugh or brush their teeth, it's simply the way they are.

Sometimes one of us may summon up the courage to ask for something different, but it is tricky. Coaching is all right for tennis, but much harder with something so personal. It isn't easy to find a way to communicate exactly what we want, and it gets even more difficult to say exactly what is wrong if our partner doesn't get it right reasonably quickly. Nor is it easy for the other person to respond appropriately. A natural reaction is to start to think about it all: 'Does she mean like this? Did she always want something different (when I thought it was OK)? Is that better? Can I remember how to do it again?' and so on. None of that does wonders for passion, and the thoughts might well be worse: 'Why can't I get it right? Oh God, I'm a failure. I'd rather stop than be humiliated.' Unfortunately, thinking about it virtually guarantees failure. It's one of those things, like riding a bicycle (an unfortunate analogy, perhaps, but it does come to mind) where you can't learn how to do it by thinking it out.

As well as all that, it would be lovely not to have to ask. We want to feel that the other person understands us so well, is so in tune with us, that they just know how we want to be touched. Indeed, we often take this as a sign of real love – and its absence as the lack of it. And what makes the whole thing more difficult, even agonizing, is that, deep down, we can't describe the kind of touch we really want because we can't even imagine it. It is a great good fortune to have been touched by someone in a way that was totally new, deeply familiar, absolutely reassuring and wildly exciting – all at the same time. You didn't know that that was what you wanted until you got it; and as soon as you did, you knew you'd been looking for it for as long as you can remember. It is the most enormous gift.

If we are given this gift, we still assume that it is some natural talent, just something the other person knows instinctively. It follows that if we aren't touching our partner in the right way, we think that we don't have that talent, and there's nothing much we can do about it. This whole attitude is based on a lack of knowledge about touch. It is perfectly possible for anyone to learn to touch their partner in a way that fulfils that deep desire.

touching the energy body

When someone has done something kind for us, especially when we neither asked for nor expected it, we say, 'I was touched.' That is what physical touch feels like when it is just right. It feels like an act of kindness which makes us feel recognized, appreciated, valued, respected. It evokes a response deep in the body and, usually, a smile. There is obviously more going on than the literal physical touch on the body, because we have all been touched countless times without experiencing any of these responses. How can a touch be touching?

To start to answer that question, I want to point out that no two people like to be touched in exactly the same way. One person likes to be handled as if he is bone china, another as if she is a boisterous puppy. When being touched, some people like quick decisive movements, others like slow languorous ones. And you can't deduce what kind of touch a person likes from talking to them or looking at them; you might imagine that well-built, strong people all like a firm touch and small thin people like a light one, but that isn't the case. A client of mine who weighs about nineteen stone likes the most delicate touch imaginable, and an almost anorexic dancer likes being touched as if she were a rugby player in a scrum. This has two important and obvious implications. The first is that, in the process of touching, you need to be in a frame of mind which is open and receptive. Your partner will convey a stream of messages about the way he or she wants to be touched which will, if they are attended to, provide an unerring guide. You can't go to sleep on the job, so to speak. Nor does this change, however long you have been with your sexual partner. For one thing, like pretty much everything else, you can always get better at it, and, for another, your partner's life has endless variations of mood and tempo; responding to these, through touch, conveys a message that you are aware of and understand what is going on for your partner and that you are there in support. If you remain willing to listen, there is scope for communicating love through touch in ever more subtle and precise ways.

It can't be the physical body alone which is involved in touch, otherwise noticing a person's size or build would tell you how he or she likes to be touched. Whenever you touch the physical body you also touch the energy body. If an energy body is light and responsive, and the touch it is given is heavy handed, the person will feel crushed, overwhelmed, even abused. If an energy body is robust and strong and the touch is light, it'll be irritating and feel like an itch or a fly crawling on the skin. When the vibration of a person's energy body is slow and steady and the touch moves fast and erratically, that person will feel he can't keep up and, like a small child left behind on a walk, will start to lose interest and finally give up altogether. If an energy body is ignored, the person feels ignored. You may recognize one of these reactions yourself. The notion of an energy body explains why a particular touch, even when given by someone who cares for you, may not feel good. It can also help all of us to touch in ways that feel wonderful.

You can touch the energy body off the skin, just on the skin or deeper in the body. The first two can be erotic, but almost all the time it is contact deeper in the body which feels best. But how deep?

If you put your hand lightly on the skin of another person and leave it resting there for a few moments you'll only get a vague impression of the shape of that part of the body which you touch and some impression of its warmth or coldness. That's not a lot of information, and in particular it won't tell you anything about how he or she wants to be touched, either generally or in a particular moment. If your partner touches you in this way, the hand won't make much impression on you. You'll be able to tell there is something resting on you, but you won't have a clear feeling of its shape or where it begins and ends. Nor will you quite know, from the feeling in your body alone, what it is that is there; it could easily be a piece of material rather than a human being. It is all rather fuzzy and uninteresting. We all want contact with the person we love, we all want to feel that he or she is connecting with us personally and individually, and we won't usually get it with this kind of light touch.

If, on the other hand, you touch very firmly you'll notice that it will be quite an effort; there will be tension in your hand and wrist, and probably right up your arm. Making such an effort keeps your concentration on yourself, and again prevents you discovering what the other person wants. The person receiving a very firm touch will probably feel squashed, as if a part of the body is being distorted by what you are doing. That will feel uncomfortable. It will be physically uncomfortable, but there is more to it than that. He or she will feel as if you are imposing some idea on that part of their body, and indeed on them as a person, rather than doing what is kind and respectful. There will be, you might say, a breakdown in communication; the hand will be doing what it is going to do irrespective of what is wanted or even acceptable.

Somewhere on the spectrum between a touch that is too light and one that is too firm is one that feels just right to the receiver, and for each of us it will come at a different place on that spectrum. It is usually nearer the firm end, because with a relatively firm touch the receiver will have the sensation that bone is being touched; not literally, of course, but in most places on the body a firm touch does bring about contact between the underlying bone of the hand and an underlying bone in the other person's body. We aren't normally aware of our bones, but bone is at the core of us and it usually feels good to be touched at that core. Because there is quite a lot of yield in the soft tissue of the body – flab is a less polite way of putting it – if the touch is only into flab you don't feel that it is making a real contact with you. When the touch is absorbed into flab its effect is dispersed rather than concentrated. If it goes through flab on to bone it feels vivid, focused, attentive. This isn't to say that fatter people necessarily need a firmer touch and thinner people a lighter one. A fat person may be highly sensitive to touch and relatively light pressure may be felt strongly in the bone or deep musculature. Equally, the muscles of a thin person may be so tense that touch bounces off, so to speak, and quite a lot of pressure is needed to overcome that resistance and get into contact with what lies deeper.

You can try this yourself, to see what depth of touch feels best for you. Start by touching the shin bone, on the inside of the leg near the front, about half-way down. Use the tip of a finger and press hard enough to get information about the bone – does it feel smooth or pitted, brittle or flexible, solid or fragile? Don't rub, but try touching in other places on the same bone to see if it is the same or different there. Now, for comparison, touch the bone of an index finger, just above the knuckle, and ask yourself similar questions. Now you know what it feels like to touch bone, try touching a rib on the upper chest, above the breast and about half-way between the shoulder and mid-line. This time, because the bone has more flesh covering it, you will have to judge how firmly to press and you will have to make your touch more deliberate to sense exactly when you are in contact with bone. This time, once you are in contact with bone notice not so much what the bone feels like but what sensations or impressions you are getting from your fingertip. Do you feel in touch with more than just the place where your finger is resting? How does the body respond to the touch? Try other places near by and try on the other side – do you get the same impressions or different ones? You can, of course, try all this with a partner. If you do, experiment with adjusting your touch so that it makes the same kind of deliberate contact that you felt when there was bone under your finger without being uncomfortable.

When you get just the right degree of pressure in your touch you will be touching your partner's energy body as well as his or her physical body. How do you know whether or not you are doing that? When you are in touch with your partner's energy body, you will feel some kind of movement under your hand. If your touch is too light you won't be in sufficient contact to feel it. If your touch is too firm you won't feel any movement either; your touch will be so strong that it will override the energy body and block out its response, like trying to hear what someone is saying to you when there is very loud music on.

The best way to describe what this movement feels like when you're touching the energy body is to say that it is like having your fingers on a hose pipe when someone turns on the tap; you can feel, through the plastic of the pipe, when water starts to flow through. This is a pretty good image because energy flows through bone and muscles in much the same way as water flows through a pipe. Another image is that the whole area of the body you are touching seems to melt, like an ice lolly on the tongue, softening and dissolving as you hold it. Or you might feel a sort of shifting, as if the bones you are touching are moving, not because of the pressure you are exerting but from some force within. You might feel a wave pass under your hands or you might feel a regular pulsing rhythm. The key point is that you will feel movement and change under your hand and, of course, it isn't the physical body which is moving.

You might feel movement not where you are touching but in another part of the body. A fisherman feels the movement of a fish taking the hook at the end of the line; a kite flyer feels a gust of wind catch the kite high above. With your hand on a knee, for example, you might feel a shift in the shoulder, or the neck. If you really are touching the energy body you'll feel that shift wherever it happens. But how, in this example, do you know it is in the shoulder or the neck? Well, sometimes you aren't sure exactly where it is, but more often it is obvious. You sense the direction from which the vibration comes to your hand, and you sense how far away it is, and you put the two together and draw the right conclusion. It's much the same as the way you can tell where a sound is coming from.

As I pointed out in the introduction, we tend, in this culture, to perceive things more easily than processes. If you think of the body as a thing, then it is easy to assume that if it isn't being deliberately moved it will have no movement. If you start with this assumption, it can take a little practice to overcome it and feel the energy body which, like a fountain, is created by movement and is always in movement. In fact, it is easy to feel the movement of the energy body under your hands, and the more you can drop your expectation of not being able to do it, the easier it becomes.

mutuality

When a person is touched in a way that feels just right, it will also feel just right for the one who is touching. What happens is a mutual accommodation of both energy bodies. This mutuality is crucial. A simple reason for this is that any strain in your touch will communicate itself to your partner, and it will make the touch feel awkward, uncomfortable and effortful. Your partner just won't be able to relax into it and enjoy it, because it feels as if it is going to collapse at any minute. This is most obvious if your partner likes a firm touch and you are straining to provide it. But the same is true if he or she wants a light one; it can be quite an effort for you to pull back, so to speak, from what feels easy and natural for you. In either case, the thing to do is not to keep on trying to do what is difficult for you, but to adjust your touch quite deliberately, as far as you comfortably can, in the direction your partner prefers. Your partner's energy body will register that change and start to adjust to the level of pressure you are providing. You will reach a place where you can both relax; in balance with each other.

This is the doorway to a delightful dance. Once you have found this basic balance, and both of your energy bodies know and trust that it can always be found, then they will also be willing to move away from it. Starting from the baseline, so to speak, of a balanced touch and secure in the knowledge that any deviation from it is not some mistake or misunderstanding, each partner can lead the other to a different kind of contact. So, for example, you can progressively lighten your touch. What usually happens then is that the experience of the touch will be much more intense than usual, as if you are both holding your breath. It is harder to maintain the balance with this new, lighter, touch so both of you have to concentrate harder to do so. With this intensity comes a kind of delicacy – the contact is rather fragile – which can feel wonderful and, among the rough and tumble of daily life, it may be exactly what the relationship has needed. What might happen instead is that your partner, unconsciously wishing to maintain the usual level of balance, may move his or her body in towards your touch. That can feel wonderful too – a kind of reaching out to you, an expressed desire to stay close. Again, this may be a particular communication which the relationship needs at that moment. These and many other possibilities open out once the two of you have established the basic balance of touch which suits you both.

There is a deeper reason why it is well worth finding this place of mutual balance and accommodation. It is because it conveys a particular message. Every time we touch we convey some kind of message, whether we are conscious of it or not. For example, a mother's touch often communicates caring and protection and it is immensely comforting, especially to a child who has fallen over and hurt himself. That kind of touch might feel good to your partner if he or she is in some distress, but it could be irritating in other circumstances. If I am angry, or insisting on saying something I think is important, and my partner touches me in that way, the message I will get is 'Dear me, what a fuss. Come here and Mummy will make it better.' Infuriating, to me at any rate; I will feel it as patronizing or controlling or smothering. It misses where I am by a mile. As it would do at a time of sexual interest and excitement.

A touch which is brusque and offhand communicates that the person isn't really interested in you, in what you want and what you are feeling. A touch which drags across the skin lasciviously may communicate, 'I am irresistible to you and I know it', which usually has the opposite effect. There is an absent-minded kind of touch; it says, 'I'm busy thinking of something else, and this should keep you happy while I get on with it.' I'm sure you can think of plenty of other examples from your own experience.

The point is that a touch which has mutuality conveys a very different message; it communicates interest and respect. It communicates a willingness to meet, to be together. And that stimulates trust. When you are touched like this, there is a kind of instinctive yielding to the touch. It's as if you can lean on it, literally and emotionally, because you know it won't let you down. As a couple start to trust each other's touch, they open more and more to each other, they reveal themselves to each other, and that allows each of them to let go of all the façades and pretences they have kept up, as we all do, and just be who they are. It is such a relief not to have to pretend or perform, or to try and be who you think the other person wants you to be. And it is such a relief not to have to pretend that the other person is who they are pretending to be. Mutuality in touch is a doorway into intimacy.

attention

To discover this kind of mutuality, and it is a discovery, there are only two things you have to do. One of them, as I have mentioned, is to contact your partner's physical and energy bodies simultaneously without strain. The other is to touch with attention. It is amazing how seldom we pay attention to what we are touching, and even more amazing what a difference it makes when we do. At the moment, you are touching this book, and perhaps something else too. Yet I'm sure you couldn't say what it felt like, what the sensations were in your fingertips. Your attention was elsewhere, so you didn't notice. As an experiment, put your attention on your fingertips now – see how much information you can pick up about what you are touching. Is it warm or cold, smooth or rough, hard or soft, uniform or varied? Are your fingers on two different surfaces, or three, or more? What's the difference between those surfaces? There is a vast amount of information there. When you touch your partner's body there is far more information available to you, because it is a living thing changing all the time, registering shifts of mood and emotion, thoughts and desires, and responding to you as well. If your attention isn't on your touch, you'll miss all this and you'll have no idea what is going on for him or her. You'll be like a blind person at an art gallery or a deaf person at a concert. You'll be like someone engaged in a long monologue, oblivious to the audience (which is bound to get restless, sooner or later, however interested it was at the beginning). If you put your attention on where you are touching, the monologue becomes a dialogue. You will be listening as well as communicating; what you want to communicate will be changed by what you are hearing, and the two of you will be collaborating.

Attention is the essence of intimacy in touch as it is in talking. When you are leaning over a dinner table, telling your partner something you think is important, interesting or just funny, and you suddenly realize that she is miles away, and has been for the past five minutes, it can be very upsetting. You might feel that you are boring, or a bit of a fool; you might blame your partner for not caring about you and what matters to you. The blame may well be inappropriate. Your partner may have switched off because you weren't paying attention to her; perhaps you didn't realize that she had been trying to talk about something that mattered to her for the past half an hour, but you had droned on with some story, whose ending she had spotted ten minutes ago. It doesn't matter how it started or who started it, there has been a breakdown of intimacy, a missing instead of a meeting, and it can feel quite devastating. It is very much the same with touch.

> . . . she turned and passed her hand through his arm.
> Mr Casaubon kept his hands behind him and allowed her pliant arm to cling with difficulty against his rigid arm.
> There was something horrible to Dorothea in the sensation which this unresponsive hardness inflicted on her. That is a strong word, but not too strong; it is in these acts called trivialities that the seeds of joy are forever wasted, until men and women look around with haggard faces at the devastation their own waste has made . . .
>
> George Eliot, *Middlemarch*[2]

I want to contrast attention with intention in touch. I once had a massage which felt awful. The masseur found some place which he thought should be different, and set about making it how he thought it ought to be. The message was 'I don't want you to be like this and I'm going to work on you until you've changed to how I know you should be – it's for your own good of course.' My body hated that. It felt criticized, vulnerable and manipulated. It responded by tensing up, which made him try even harder to change me. I ended up feeling battered. To a lesser extent this is what tends to happen if you have a specific intention when you touch your partner. It is all right to have a sort of general intention – to re-establish the connection between the two of you or to give your partner pleasure. But if you have a specific intention – to excite your partner, or relax him, make him feel cherished, or appreciate what a wonderful lover you are – it doesn't work. You'll start imposing on him rather than being with him, he'll resist in some way, and the touch will create a gulf between the two of you. On the other hand if you stick to simply paying attention and focus on the point of contact between you, there will be a sensation of joining and meeting. Attention is in your hands, or whichever part of you is doing the touching, but intentions are in your head. You can woo someone with your head, but you make love with your body.

What you are doing when you touch your partner with attention is simply being present. That sounds like a damp squib of a conclusion, but it isn't. Hardly any of us is present hardly any of the time. We are busy thinking about a conversation we had last week, remembering that we have to take something to the cleaners so it is ready for the weekend, worrying about one of the children, thinking through a problem at work, wondering where to go on holiday. On and on it goes, a state of more or less permanent distraction. So familiar is this that it is almost a shock to suddenly find oneself present; as we are when we are fully absorbed in a piece of music, a view, a task or a touch. The shock is a kind of recognition; we remember that this is how it is to live fully, and realize that all the rest of the time we haven't been doing so. Paying attention organizes the energy body; you get intensity and relaxation at the same time. Another way of putting it is to say that there is no disjunction between the mind and body, as there is when we do one thing while thinking about another. You can see it when top-class athletes are competing – they call it being in the 'zone', and they know that in that state they can do what is normally impossible.

To sum up what I have said so far, when you touch the physical body and the energy body together, with attention, then there is scope for an extraordinary variety of touch. With that variety at your fingertips you will create an immensely powerful and infinitely subtle form of relationship with your partner; one that enables you to meet in ways that you may never have met before.

variety

What most people do without realizing it is to touch in such a way that their energy bodies blend together. Think of two pieces of chocolate – one dark, one milk – left out in the sun, melting together when they touch. Similarly at the place where two energy bodies meet, they can lose their separate boundaries and melt into each other.[3] Normally, this kind of blending feels lovely. Most people's earliest experience is of lying in a mother's arms, nourished, safe and warm, and that memory becomes an ideal they try to find again. All lovers want to blend with their loved one in an embrace, perhaps because it evokes this infant bliss, perhaps because each wants to be a part of the other, certainly because it is a source of deep pleasure. The two people lose their sense of separateness when their energy bodies blend together.

> After when they disentwine
> You from me and yours from mine
> Neither can be certain who
> Was that I whose mine was you.
> To the act again they go
> More completely not to know.
> Robert Graves, *from* 'The Thieves'[4]

Blending with someone you love and trust can leave you feeling stronger and more whole than before. What happens is that the two of you have found a way to create an energy body which is more organized and more coherent than the energy body of either. Imagine that where yours is weak your partner's is strong, where yours is flowing freely your partner's is blocked; putting the two together enables each of you to draw on the other's strengths. To live within that energy body for a while feels good, may free you from the limitations you normally experience and may leave your energy body in a better state than before.

But there is another option. It is to touch in such a way that the energy bodies of the two people remain distinct, but they resonate together. The word 'resonate' has a specific scientific meaning; here I am using it in the everyday sense as 'a response in parallel or sympathy' (*Oxford English Dictionary*). Through touch, each of the separate energy bodies evokes a sympathetic response from the other. The difference between this and blending is that when the energy bodies blend 'Neither can be certain who/Was that I whose mine was you'; but when they resonate together each can be certain who. By analogy, it's the difference between two violins playing the same note with the same expression, or any two instruments playing two different notes a perfect fifth apart (an interval which sounds harmonious to the human ear). In the latter case the separateness of each note and each instrument is obvious, indeed the contrast between the two notes is striking and enlivening, but they go well together and complement each other.

So when two people touch they can create a blending of their energy bodies or a mutual resonance between them. Given that blending feels so good, why look for an alternative? There are a number of situations when a different kind of touch, which I will call interface touch, is valuable. This touch maintains the boundaries between the two energy bodies; they meet at interface, and that allows them to resonate together. If you are in a new relationship and feel a little unsure about your partner, then blending has disadvantages. Your own energy body will be altered by the experience of blending and you may find it difficult to re-establish it afterwards; you might feel uncomfortable, awkward, disorientated. People often try to express this by saying that they 'don't feel themselves', which sounds vague but is entirely accurate. They don't feel themselves; instead they are feeling their new and altered energy body. When a person has sexual relations with a number of partners in a relatively short space of time, and blends with the energy bodies of each of them, this problem can become acute. There will have been so many changes in that person's energy body that he or she really can lose a sense of self. It might feel a little like wearing a very ill-assorted set of clothes – the trousers are far too short, the shirt is far too big, the hat is far too tight and the colours all clash. And because that person doesn't realize what has happened they can neither prevent it happening nor put it right once it has happened.

Interface touch is also valuable if, for some reason, you are no longer finding the interest and excitement you used to feel from your partner's touch – the chances are that you have been blending for some time and have become so accustomed to it that it feels as ordinary and as boringly familiar as an old jacket; comfortable and easy to slip into, but not much more. Equally, you might try it if you are finding it difficult to get close at all. Perhaps your partner has suddenly become extremely successful at work while you are going through a lean time where nothing you do seems to bear fruit, and that has altered the dynamic of the relationship (there will be more about this kind of change in chapter six). In that case, as a couple, you may have lost your ability to merge. Given the changes you have both been through, both of your energy bodies may well have changed too and it may not be possible to walk the well-worn path to blending. This may be a time when it is important to acknowledge the differences between you instead of trying to submerge them, and creating resonance may be a route to a new and refreshing form of intimacy. Finally, touching without blending may be vital if there is inequality in the relationship which is resented by one or both of you. In this case, the likelihood is that one person's energy body is predominating in the merged energy body. While that is going on it will be extremely difficult for the partner with the weaker energy body to assert him or herself in the relationship. However many deliberate and well-intentioned efforts he or she makes in other areas of life, they will be undermined and subverted in bed. Whatever is done in the daytime to create equality, the dominance of one partner will be re-established each night in the closeness of sex and sleep.

The difference between a touch which leads to blending and a touch which maintains an interface between the two energy bodies, and allows resonance, is a matter of degree. The lighter the touch the easier it is to blend: or, to say the same thing in a different way, the harder it is to maintain an interface. Next, the longer you maintain contact in one place, or on one area of the body, the easier it is to blend. The reason for this is that as time goes by your attention tends to slip on to something other than the touch, and as it slips away so does your awareness of the boundary between you. And, for the same basic reason, the greater the area touched the easier it is to blend; there are so many points of contact that it is hard to maintain attention on all of them.

To experiment with touching at interface, start as follows. With a fingertip only, touch your partner's lower arm on either the inside or the outside edge – where you can feel the bone easily. Make your touch deep enough so that you are aware of the bone under your finger, and keep your attention firmly focused on the exact point of contact between you. Notice how that feels and ask your partner how it feels too: adjust your touch if it seems too light or too firm. Now try doing the same on your partner's back, about half-way between the centre and the side; it is a bit more difficult to feel bone here, but you should be able to locate a rib and have the sensation that you are touching it. Do the same with a rib on the upper chest at the front; you'll probably find that here you need less pressure to contact the underlying bone, and that your partner will feel the effect of the touch more deeply. Once you've got the basic idea you can use three or four fingers and you can see how it feels to touch underlying bone in other places – for example on the pelvis. What is the same wherever you touch and however much of your own body you use to touch is the quality of attention which is needed. If you can't keep your awareness clearly on the whole of the contact between the two of you, you won't be able to maintain interface touch. At first, as with any new skill, it takes quite a lot of concentration, but quite quickly you'll find that it becomes natural and effortless.

Although the distinction between blending and interface is a matter of degree, they feel very different. With a blending touch, you lose awareness both of your body and of your partner's; the boundaries dissolve and a rather vague and dreamy sensation takes over. It's a bit like the time just after you've woken from a deep sleep and you aren't quite sure where you are or who you are. With an interface touch you become acutely aware of yourself and the other as separate and different. And, of course, in sexual contact, difference is exciting. There is a heightened sense of the qualities both of your own body and your partner's – shape, skin texture, softness or hardness, movement, areas of tension and so on – and a remarkable clarity of sensations and emotions which the contact is stimulating in you.

The way in which two partners touch each other has profound consequences for their relationship. It can be a source of frustration, indifference and disharmony, and these are bound to affect other areas of the couple's shared life. On the other hand, discovering ways to touch that really suit you both can lead to new levels of trust and communication between you, an increased sensitivity to each other's nature and much more sheer pleasure. Difficulties between the two of you which you have not managed to resolve through talking are amenable to change through touch. I am thinking, mainly, of relationships where there are unresolved power issues. If, for example, the relationship suffers because one partner finds it hard to surrender to the other and finds cause to argue and object even when there is nothing much at stake, then a touch which really suits that person, which asserts respect and acceptance, may make it easy for him or her to yield to it and let go of some old defences against yielding. With that experience of surrender, and the knowledge that it was safe and pleasurable, it may be possible to let go of the habitual resistance which has set up a dynamic of confrontation. I am thinking too of cases where, because of disparities of wealth or beauty, or sheer force of personality, one partner assumes a dominant role and the other a subservient one. Sometimes the two people are both content to remain in those roles, but more often the disparity is a source of anxiety and discontent.

Above all, the nature of a person's touch is not invariant or invariable. Trying out different kinds of touch may feel a little awkward at first, but the rewards can be the re-energizing of a relationship and its launch into new and surprising intimacy.

chapter three

getting together

Let's say that any organ in the body has its energy impulse, an impulse to action, and the experience of the conflicts of these different energies inside is what constitutes the psyche. It's nature talking.

Joseph Campbell, *The Hero's Journey*[1]

After a time, a new relationship starts to acquire a degree of stability. The two people begin to feel some commitment to each other, may introduce their respective family and friends to each other, and find that they are sharing their lives. At about this time they may become aware of a tension between two opposing pressures. On the one hand, the partners are two separate people – each with his or her own personality, needs and desires – who need to preserve their individuality. The relationship won't flourish if one partner's personality, needs and desires are subsumed to those of the other. On the other hand, the relationship won't be intimate and fulfilling if the two of them just go their separate ways and meet up to carry out day-to-day tasks, if they live together, or to have holidays, if they live apart. Somehow, the couple have to find a way of dealing with the dilemma of being both separate and together.

As the couple encounter this dilemma for the first time, differences between the two of them may highlight it. If one partner is naturally sociable, likes the sense of another person's presence in the house, enjoys talking late into the night, he or she will expect and encourage the shared life. If the other is quiet and reserved, likes his or her own company, he or she will tend to try and preserve the separate lives. The dilemma may become severe when one partner is in the grip of a strong emotion. Anger is particularly difficult. If it is your partner who is angry, your choice seems to be between two unattractive options: staying aloof, apparently unmoved, or joining in and escalating it into a full-blown row. Other emotions aren't easy either. It can be tricky if your partner is grieving for something or someone but you aren't. To stay separate from your partner's emotion seems unkind and unfriendly, as if you are washing your hands of him or her. On the other hand, if you try to join in with that emotion, you may feel awkward and hypocritical, or perhaps overwhelmed by its force.

What usually happens is that, over time, the two people find some mutual accommodation between separateness and intimacy; an accommodation which works in the sense that it is a compromise of some kind which causes neither of them too much distress. They would like it to be better than that but they can't seem to change it – or daren't risk trying for fear of losing what they've got. In fact, it is relatively easy to change, and there is no risk involved. It doesn't require the agonizing excavation of old hurts and buried hopes, doesn't need the re-enactment of childhood experiences with parents and siblings – important and interesting as they are – and doesn't take years of sustained effort. What it does take is some knowledge of the anatomy and physiology of energy, which is described in this chapter, and a willingness to explore the energy of your relationship. As for all explorers, whether the buccaneers who first sailed from Europe to the Americas, or the twentieth-century scientists who explored the world of quantum physics, there will be some surprises because you will be in unknown territory.

emotions as energy

Medical science distinguishes a considerable number of sub-systems in the body. The skeleton and muscles are seen as one sub-system, as is the circulation of the blood, the endocrine system and so on. These systems interact. For example, blood carries hormones around the body and the action of the muscles helps blood flow back from the extremities to the heart. The anatomy and physiology of energy is at least as complicated and at least as interconnected. But for the purposes of this chapter we are concerned first with the energy of the organs in general and then with the energy of the heart in particular.[2]

Each of the organs has a specialized function carried out by specialized cells; a cell in the liver is different from a cell in the heart or the spleen. In the light of this, it is not surprising that each organ has a different kind of energy. In Chinese thought, each of the energies of the organs is associated with particular aspects of the natural world. The energy of the liver is linked to plant life and to springtime, and is forceful, outgoing, active, initiating; it rises up the body and comes out in a sudden sharp tone of voice and abrupt movements. I once planted a climbing rose at the foot of a tall pine tree. For four years the rose seemed dormant, possibly dead. The fifth year, in the spring, it grew thirty feet or more right up into and through the branches of the tree. I could almost sit and watch it grow. That is an expression of the energy of the liver; or, to put it more accurately, of the particular kind of energy in the world which animates both the rose and the liver alike.

When I experience this kind of energy in me I think of it as an emotion and call it anger. Anger bursts out of me – unless I make the considerable effort of holding it in. It has that upwards and outwards force to it. I notice the same thing when I'm on the receiving end of someone else's anger. I remember being confronted by an angry woman. Her face went red, which was the energy rising up in her; she shouted at me and jabbed her pointed finger towards my face, which was that energy coming outwards. As all this energy came out towards me I felt attacked by its force.

To take a different example of emotion as energy, I remember grieving for a friend who died. My chest caved in, my face went white as colour drained out of it, my voice became weak and tearful. I was exhausted. I felt as if I was collapsing inwards. I wanted to be in my own home and to be left alone. In short, what we call the emotions can be seen as manifestations of energy; in fact, this idea is contained in the word 'emotion' which means, literally, 'movement away from'. With anger it is movement away from the centre outwards; with grief, it is movement away from the extremities to the centre.

Each emotion, then, can be seen as a particular quality of energy associated with a particular organ. It may seem a rather trivial matter of semantics to re-label the emotions as energy, but it opens up all new ways of dealing constructively and creatively with emotions in a relationship. When one partner feels a strong emotion, it usually evokes an automatic response from the other. If your partner is angry with you, which way do you jump? Do you fight back, placate, sulk or let it wash over you? If your partner feels a lot of fear and anxiety about life, do you sympathize, get protective, collect tranquillizers from the chemist, become impatient or what? Whatever you do will generate a reaction in your partner – and off you'll go together down what is probably a well-worn path. It may be a good path to be on; maybe you have found a way of reacting which helps your partner and helps the two of you to come through it together. But if you haven't, if times of heightened emotion are difficult for you both and tend to drive you apart, then it will be useful to have an alternative response. One alternative is to learn to see your partner's emotion as an energy, and to respond to it energetically yourself.

This is not difficult. The first, and most important, thing you need to do is to stay at interface. In the previous chapter I explained the idea of interface in the context of touch; but it goes wider than that. The kernel of the idea is that you stay aware of the boundary between the two of you, the place where your energy body meets your partner's, and that the two energy bodies do not merge or blend together. You can stay at interface emotionally in pretty much the same way as you can stay at interface while touching. It is the way to preserve separateness while being together. If you can maintain an interface between your partner's emotions and your own, between your two energies, then however intertwined your lives become each of you can preserve your sense of identity and your personal space.

The energy body of a person who is feeling a strong emotion will have a powerful quality to it. Instead of it being a composite, a product of the different vibrations of the different organs, just one vibration will predominate. It'll be like all the instruments of an orchestra playing exactly the same notes together – or even playing the same note relentlessly. Diversity and variety have been replaced by a focused, rigid uniformity. There is only one message, and nothing else will be apparent to either of you. You may know that he or she cares for you, for example, but for the time being neither of you can hear or feel that. If you are not feeling the same emotion as your partner, or you are feeling it to a much lesser extent, the chances are that your energy body will be swamped. The pointed force of your partner's energy will overwhelm yours. What is more, with many emotions, you will naturally tend to join in anyway as a gesture of support, understanding and affection.

If you join your partner in her emotion, in her energy state, you'll be of no real use to her. Thomas Merton, who was a Trappist monk and writer, used the following analogy to explain why.[3] If someone falls into a river which is in flood, and is struggling to keep his head above water, the best thing you can do is to stay on the bank, get a firm hold on a tree and throw him a rope. It really won't help if you jump in too; he needs you to save him, not to drown with him. Jumping in with him is the equivalent of allowing yourself to join your partner in his energetic state; staying on the bank and throwing a rope is staying at interface. The reason why this analogy seems to me such a good one is that being in the grip of a strong emotion is very like being swept away by a flood – that overwhelming tide of feeling which you can neither resist nor deny.

Staying at interface doesn't mean being uninterested, detached, indifferent or unsympathetic to your partner's plight. It just means maintaining a separation between your two energies. You can do that while being full of love and compassion for the person and her predicament; actually more full than if you get caught up in her emotional state. That's because to stay at interface you have to give your partner your full attention. It's the same as with touch. If you intend anything – intend your partner to feel better, to get it all out, to pull herself together, to stop criticizing you, whatever the intention – you won't be at interface. The same is true if you have an intention for yourself; an intention to show her how much you care, or an intention to find the right words to calm her down, or to show her that you're unaffected by her histrionics. Any of these intentions will stop you being at interface and lead to a blending of your energy bodies, and hence to a merging of your emotional states. Your intention will change her energy state, and that change will, in turn, change yours – and the process will continue until neither of you will quite know what's going on and both of you will feel a bit lost in some quagmire together. I'm sure you've experienced the way that couples wind themselves up until both partners are in the same state – I certainly have. But if you simply put all your attention on what she is going through, you're staying on the bank and throwing a rope. When she is ready, not when you intend her to be ready, she can catch hold of it and there is someone at the other end to help pull her out.

In her book *A Life of One's Own*, first published in 1934, psychoanalyst Marion Milner discovered the difference between attention and intention, and learned to use it quite deliberately.

> . . . it occurred to me that there must be two quite different ways of perceiving. Only a tiny act of will was necessary to pass from one to the other, yet this act seemed sufficient to change the face of the world . . . The first way of perceiving seemed to be the automatic one, the kind of attention which my mind gave to everyday affairs when it was left to itself . . . The second way of perceiving seemed to occur when . . . there was no need to select one item to look at rather than another, so it became possible to look at the whole at once. To attend

to something yet want nothing from it, these seemed to be the essentials of the second way of perceiving . . . once when ill in bed, so fretting with unfulfilled purpose that I could not at all enjoy the luxury of enforced idleness, I had found myself staring vacantly at a faded cyclamen and happened to remember to say to myself, 'I want nothing.' Immediately I was so flooded with the crimson of the petals that I thought I had never before known what colour was.

Marion Milner, *A Life of One's Own*[1]

Staying at interface with your partner is a way of dropping into 'the second way of perceiving' and it often has the same kind of outcome; even if she is looking rather faded, you are flooded with her presence and may think you have never before known what she looked like.

A good way of learning how to stay at interface is to develop the skill of really listening to your partner; you can only really listen if you give him or her your full attention. You have to be disciplined. Most obviously, you mustn't interrupt; if you start to speak, your attention will be on what you want to say and how you want to say it. Nor should you look away from your partner's eyes; if you do you are bound to be distracted. Try to be passive; we all have a thousand ways of telling our partner what we think without using words. The lifted eyebrow, the tiny frown, the short 'um' noise of agreement (different from the long 'uummm' which usually means that you think what has been said isn't quite right) are all expressions of your intention, instructing the speaker to say more about this topic, avoid that subject, and so on.

Sooner or later, you'll notice that your attention has wandered. You'll have some reaction to what your partner has just said and find a thought like 'Why don't you . . . ?' or 'I'm not sure you're right about that' or 'I'm sorry that has happened to you' taking your attention. Or maybe you just drift off and start to think about something at work or something you forgot to do yesterday. It's bound to happen; just notice it as quickly as possible and find a way of re-focusing your attention on your partner. The trick I use is to imagine myself picking up the thought and laying it down on the floor beside me; if my partner talks for more than a few minutes I end up with a row of thoughts alongside my chair, all neatly lined up.

You can also get into the habit of staying at interface when you're talking to your partner. Not when you're saying something trivial, but when you're talking about something important which involves you both. Try to use only 'I' and not 'you'. It seems impossible, but it isn't. Instead of saying, 'You were an hour late when I'd specially asked you to be on time for the party; you're always late', rephrase it as, 'I felt very upset on Friday evening when I waited for an hour to go to the party.' Although this seems like a rather tortuous semantic procedure, there is a real benefit to it. Using this simple device allows you see that what your partner did or didn't do, and the way you reacted to it, are separate issues. How you respond amounts to a choice on your part.

To sum up so far, relationships can become bogged down and limiting when the couple can't maintain some separation between the two of them. It is most acute when they merge or blend their emotional states. When both of them get stuck in anger together, for example, the very existence of the relationship can be threatened. But being stuck in joy can be just as bad, in its way. In this case, the couple have a tacit agreement that they are happy as can be, life is wonderful, and neither of them can imagine wanting anything they haven't got. Sooner or later one partner will feel sad, depressed, frustrated, will cease to want the things he wanted before, and so on – it happens to everyone, it's part of normal life. And feeling these things means that the person's energy will be, and will need to be, withdrawn, quiet, pensive. But if the relationship is stuck in joy, that won't be acceptable; it will be a breach of the contract, so to speak. In those circumstances, people respond with all sorts of repressions and denials, which can be so effective that they don't even know what they're feeling any more. The long-term consequences can be awful. Pent-up feelings can erupt many years later, with dramatic suddenness, as some apparently trivial incident breaks the dam which is holding them all back. Or a person may end up so cut off from her true feelings that she loses all sense of what she wants from her life – which then becomes a meaningless round of what has to be done. There are many variants, most of which manifest as illness or depression in middle age. And, meanwhile, the relationship starves to death for want of real emotion.

the heart

I turn now to the other side of the tension between being separate and being together; where the issue is that the two people find it difficult to be intimate with each other. Symptoms of this state are that they may choose to spend their spare time in the company of friends, that when they are alone together they tend to be busy on some task; they may even find themselves organizing their work so that they aren't at home at the same time. In these circumstances, it isn't easy for them to relate to each other from the heart, which is the route to intimacy.

Normally, the heart rules the body. This is not some woolly and sentimental wishful thinking. A heartbeat sends vibrations of sound throughout the body. Put your ear on your partner's chest, just below the left breast, and you'll hear it quite clearly. Given that the body is largely composed of water, and water is an excellent conductor of sound waves, this rhythmic 'lub-dub' sound radiates out from the heart and through every cell. Somewhat like a metronome, it sets the basic tempo of all the myriad internal flows and processes of the body. What is more, early in the twentieth century it was discovered that each heartbeat starts with a pulse of electricity; that is what stimulates the contraction of the muscle of the heart which in turn pumps blood. This electrical pulse is so strong that it can be detected anywhere and everywhere in the body, even on the skin of the toes. At that time scientists realized that this electrical pulse would create a magnetic field in the surrounding area, but for the next sixty years there were no measuring devices sufficiently sophisticated to pick it up. When it was finally measured, it was discovered that this magnetic field extends well beyond the physical boundary of the body. In other words, through the magnetic field which it creates, the heart has a widespread effect not only on the whole body but on others who are near enough to sense it. The brain produces a similar, but much less powerful field; in fact, all the organs create a magnetic field, but that of the heart is by far the strongest.[5]

I talked earlier about the fact that each organ has its own particular vibration, its own 'impulse to action', to use the words of the heading quotation. The vibration of the heart gives us feelings of love and compassion for others and generates a sense of oneness with them. If other vibrations are not especially prominent, the natural dominance of the heart's vibrations can reassert itself over the whole of the energy body. It then becomes easy and natural to relate to others with love and to seek intimacy with them. And those who are physically near enough can be affected and start to respond similarly. The two people get 'on the same wavelength', and it is a wavelength of love.

In order to explain the implications of this, and how it works, I want to start by pointing out that we all know that our own heart can feel heavy or light, full of joy or of sorrow, that it can reach out to another or feel closed and inaccessible. These experiences are energetic. That is, the physical entity we call the heart isn't heavier or fuller, but as it vibrates faster or slower or as its field expands or contracts, we notice the change. If you pay attention, you will notice the state of the energetic field of another person's heart. There are thousands of tiny signs which convey that information – gestures, the amount of eye contact, the tone of voice. Take a simple question like 'Do you really want to do that?' It can be said in such a way that it means, 'You must be a complete idiot to even consider doing that' or 'I know it's hard but I'll support you all the way if you want to do it.' The difference between them is an expression of the energy of the heart. You can pick this up without any signs by noticing the feelings which others evoke in you, for example whether you feel drawn towards them or pushed away by them. Even lying quietly in bed in the dark, without touching, it is obvious whether our partner is feeling anxious or contented, loving or hostile. In this kind of situation people often say that they are 'out of synch' with each other, and I think that is a very accurate description of what is happening.

In scientific language, synchronization has a specific meaning; here I am using it in the looser sense defined by the *Oxford English Dictionary* as 'to keep time with, go at the same rate, have co-incident periods'. If you think of vibrations as waves, then they may keep time through having an identical waveform, as in figure 2a. This represents two very similar energy bodies. There may be synchronization even though there is a marked difference between the two wave forms, as in figure 2b. Here, the two energy bodies are very compatible, even though one is louder, more dramatic and volatile than the other. Vibrations can also 'keep time' with each other even though there are differences in their rhythm, as in figure 2c, where the highs and lows of the different waves coincide regularly.

> Intimate relationship itself is accounted for in quantum terms by the overlapping of one person's wave function with that of another . . . Two people who are in the same state, for instance, will have a more harmonious intimate relationship than two people who are in a different state, as the wave fronts of their personalities meet in superpositions, on top of the other, or one entangles with the other more or less harmoniously.
>
> Danah Zohar, *The Quantum Self* [6]

As this quotation suggests, vibrations can get out of synch – the remaining parts of figure 2 give some examples. With figure 2d it is easy to imagine that

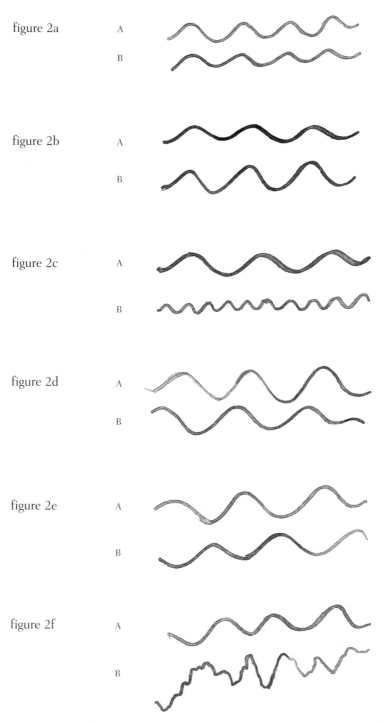

figure 2a

figure 2b

figure 2c

figure 2d

figure 2e

figure 2f

A

B

figure 2

the two people might be a little uncomfortable together; probably B would feel as if he was always trying to catch up, in some way. The situation in figure 2e would be tremendously frustrating to live with; just when A feels high, B feels low, and vice versa. They would be like two people living at opposite ends of a street – as each walks to where the other lives they meet, briefly, as they cross, but they never manage to be in the same house at the same time. The situation represented by figure 2f is even worse. Here there is a tension, almost an antagonism between the two rhythms. Perhaps you recognize some of these ways of being out of synch; I've been in all of them at one time or another.

When two energy bodies, two hearts, are mildly out of synch, each of you will feel that you are not quite well with each other, but attempts to re-establish closeness seem to miss. The hand on the arm, offered in affection, doesn't evoke an immediate softening in reply. The question about your partner's work, meant to demonstrate a spirit of collaboration, only gets a brief, flat answer. You are both trying to reignite the love, but the pilot light won't catch. When two hearts are badly out of synch (there is more on this in the next chapter) the two energy bodies seem actively to resist each other.

Although we are good at collecting this information about the state of the heart, which is so vital for the maintenance of a relationship, we may not use it well to make things better. Perhaps that's because we tend to put our attention on the content of the relationship rather than its energy. The following example explains what I mean.

She has been away from home for ten days and he has agreed to meet her at the airport. It's been a long journey for her. The plane arrives on time, but he isn't at the gate when she comes out; in fact he is half an hour late. Some people couldn't care less about this kind of thing, but she does. The whole business of him being on time is an issue between them – in fact it is bigger than that; the whole business of him not doing what he said he was going to do is an issue between them. As usual, when this kind of thing happens, they start to talk about what happened. He explains why he was late; she starts to quiz him on his explanation, which looks feebler and feebler the more questions she asks. Then he starts to talk about the time they made the arrangement in the first place, saying that he made it clear that she would arrive at a difficult time for him and suggesting she take a later plane or get a taxi from the airport. In fact, he was busy when they talked about it and had only agreed to meet her because he wanted to get on with what he was doing and didn't want the whole thing to escalate into some drama. As most couples know, this approach doesn't often bring them closer together; it usually stores up ammunition for future fights.

Instead of looking at the content of the situation, they might look at it energetically. When she came into the arrivals hall she was excited, really looking forward to seeing him again and pleased at the prospect of being together, eager for a welcoming hug. Her heart was open and expanded, vibrating powerfully. She looked for his face in the crowd, keyed up for the moment when she would spot him. In fact she stayed keyed up for longer than her mind told her was reasonable. Then, when she finally accepted that he wasn't there, all that excitement ebbed away. Her background tiredness from the journey flooded over her. Trying to force herself to think what to do next instead, she realized she felt hurt, let down; old feelings of being abandoned and uncared for rose up in her. Her heart closed and contracted – not literally, but energetically.

As for him, for the past hour he realized he was running late. He knew he should have left earlier. He fretted in a traffic jam. When he got to a clear stretch of road he started to drive much too fast, hunched over the wheel, looking out for cops, imagining the angry reception he would get when he arrived. Mixed in with all that was a kind of resentful self-justification. He was always putting himself out for her, and he always ended up worse off than if he hadn't bothered in the first place. His heart was anxious, agitated and defended – again not literally but energetically. When the two of them finally met their hearts did not.

All couples get into this kind of a state with each other sometimes. If they can talk it through in such a way that they both feel satisfied with the outcome, then that process will change the vibration of their hearts and of their energy bodies and all will be well. But many couples don't manage to get that far. In the midst of daily life they don't have the time for a long discussion. If they leave it until they do have the time, they've probably each spent the intervening hours or days digging themselves into justifications for their behaviour, and when they do talk they start to defend these fossilized positions. It's all become old and hard and stale. Perhaps they prefer to sweep the problem under the carpet anyway, or they have got into the habit of just feeling resentful and staying polite with each other. A quicker and easier route back to intimacy may be to restore some kind of harmony between the two energy bodies – never mind, for now at any rate, who did what or why. Given that the vibration of the heart dominates the energy body, this means getting the vibrations of their two hearts back in synch.

To see how this might be done, I'll take up the airport story again. After giving him a peck on the cheek, she starts to stride away through the concourse. He hates it when she does that; can't bear that bossy, rather affected way she often has about her. But somehow he also wants to make things right between them. He calls to her and says, 'Hold on. We need to stop and get together again. No good driving . . .' It feels risky, and he can't finish the sentence. There is a pause. She looks at him, crumpled, dishevelled and anxious. For a moment she wants to say, 'For heaven's sake! It's late and I'm tired, and I just want to get home.' It would be true and it would also have the advantage of making it clear that it's really his fault that she's saying 'no'. But with a distinct effort she resists the temptation and says, 'All right.'

They find a place to sit, in a corner away from the bustle. They swing some chairs round so they can sit facing each other, rather than side by side. For the first five minutes or so they just pay attention to their breathing, eyes closed. They both start to calm down. Five minutes more and she opens her eyes. She notices that their breathing has become synchronized. His eyes are still shut, so she can look at him carefully without having to meet his eyes. He looks quite young; she sees worry and a desire to please in his face. She closes her eyes again and puts her attention on to her heart. After a few moments she can feel it beating, strongly, evenly and slowly; she realizes what a contrast this is to the jerky rhythm it had when she was waiting. Feeling reassured by this, as if she's got something back she had lost, she instinctively reaches out a hand to him. At the touch they both open their eyes. He looks surprised, but he takes her hand without hesitation. She smiles and, so as not to force the pace – something she knows she does in the relationship – she closes her eyes again. They sit like that for another ten minutes.

Then he squeezes her hand. She opens her eyes to find him looking at her. She grins rather ruefully and squeezes his hand back. They both know perfectly well that this means, 'Sorry; and I'm done now, ready to go.' They get up and walk to the car. On the way home they talk about what they've each been doing while they were apart. They know it's too soon to talk about the incident itself.

Of course this is only one possible outcome; they might have driven home in a cold fury. But it is a plausible one, because it is based on the way energy works. Paying attention to the breath calms the heart. And if partners sit quietly together for ten minutes or so it is highly likely that the rhythms of their breath and their heartbeats will become synchronized. Scientists call this phenomenon 'entrainment'. On a longer time scale, it's what happens when women live and work together; after a few months their menstrual cycles become synchronized. Through entrainment, the vibrations of the two hearts come together and then it becomes much easier for either partner to feel empathy for the other. He can appreciate how disappointed she was (he realizes that she actually was looking forward to seeing him – when he was angry he thought she saw him as a superior taxi service). He understands that this makes her brittle and sharp. She realizes that he struggles with a conflict between wanting to care for her and feeling resentment at her demands – she admits she is demanding. She sees how tricky a line this is to walk. Each feels more open to the other and more compassionate. Then it becomes easy to feel loving again.

It is worth noticing that for things to work out well they both had to make an effort. He risked being slapped down and rejected, she nearly reacted that way, and she overcame her reluctance to co-operate with his idea and to stay any longer in the airport. They both chose to put energy into the relationship at a time when they were both tempted not to. It is that small but significant investment of energy that kick-starts the process.

At its simplest, all that is required in getting two hearts back in synch is that one partner is able to get calm and quiet enough for the energy of the heart to start to take over his or her energy body and that the other partner is willing to allow his or her own energy body to be affected by that. That is a simple solution, but not necessarily an easy one. For both of them what is required is focused attention.

> . . . energy has certain tendencies. The moment we look for one of those tendencies, it manifests itself, while all other tendencies remain latent . . . One might say that energy knows when it is being watched, and it behaves to fulfil our expectations. Energy responds to us.
>
> Eliot Cowan, *Plant Spirit Medicine*[7]

The one who starts the ball rolling has to put his attention on his heart; to become aware of where it is, to notice its beat, to feel how fast or slow it is, how strong or weak. There is a widespread belief that we can't feel our internal organs: it isn't true, but it does take a bit of practice. Luckily, the heart is the easiest of all to feel. And paying attention to it will start to change its vibration; it will become stronger, probably slower and more regular. He'll feel that as a resurgence of affection, in spite of whatever has happened. As for the other partner, she has to pay attention to her own energy body. If she does, she'll notice that it will start to change in response; the vibration of her heart will start to fall into synch with his. Of course, she can ignore it or even resist it simply by keeping his attention on some other vibration, such as anger, resentment or fear. But if she is willing to notice the change and to allow it to continue, the two of them will find themselves coming back into harmony.

If the couple choose to collaborate in this process they can speed it up a good deal by putting their attention on their hearts simultaneously. It also goes much faster if there is some physical contact between them; holding one hand works well, holding both works better. It is certainly possible for one partner to get the process underway without the other's co-operation – there is more on this later – but it works much more slowly.

energy and personality

It is normal to assume that relationship problems are caused by a clash of personalities; that is, a clash about needs, desires, hopes and expectations – most of them rooted in past experience – and in particular about whose are being met and whose aren't. When a couple have a problem which isn't resolved easily or at all, then, the common assumption goes, it is because unmet needs and expectations have constellated around a particular event. In the example I have just used, her need and expectation of being met at the airport clashed with his need not to feel that he was at her beck and call. Hence the way to resolve the issue is to bring these needs and expectations to consciousness; once each partner is aware of them, then he or she can choose whether to continue to live from them. That is certainly possible, but it is an awfully slow route to change. In the short term something has to be done to change a way of life together which has become unsatisfying or loveless.

One of the ways that can be done is to work with energy; and specifically with the fact that the vibration of our hearts, which dominates the energy body as a whole, can be changed. You don't have to try to change your partner, get him or her to agree with you, even find some agreed compromise between your two positions. If your two hearts, and therefore your two energy bodies, are vibrating in harmony then, at worst, the content of the personality clash is much easier to resolve. At best it is simply irrelevant.

This may seem a remarkable claim, but that is only because we take the idea of personality so seriously in this culture. We invest it with an enormous amount of power, in particular the power to explain everything about what we do and why we do it. But it is only one way of looking at human behaviour, one partial view. It is probably true that if the personalities of the partners become more compatible, then the energy between the couple will improve. It is at least as sensible to do it the other way round – if the energy of the relationship improves, the personalities become more compatible.

To conclude, I have put forward two basic ideas in this chapter which might seem to be utterly inconsistent. One is that it is important to stay at interface with your partner, not to get drawn into his or her emotional state. The other is that it is important to allow the vibrations of your separate energy bodies to become synchronized and harmonious. Are they really inconsistent? If deep intimacy does not depend on the compatibility of personalities, if it is more a matter of getting the personalities out of the way so that your natural energies are more available to each other, then perhaps intimacy and separateness aren't in opposition. The paradox – perhaps it is only a paradox because we don't understand energy very well – is that the more you stay at interface the more clearly and strongly your two energies can meet in harmony.

chapter four

conflict

I went to my lama and told him everything I was feeling. Everything. I spared him nothing. I was angry, insulting, eloquent. He listened carefully. Sometimes he would ask me to make myself clearer, to be more precise. Why did I despise him exactly? What precisely had failed me in his teaching? And so on. At the end of my tirade he said nothing. Then he looked up and said, 'Is that all?' I lost my temper. 'Is that all? I have been telling you about my deepest feelings, I have been speaking to you out of the heart of my life and you say is that all?' He smiled and said, 'Charles, being angry is the one honest thing you have done all year.'

Andrew Harvey, *Journey to Ladakh*[1]

Imagine that being in a relationship is like being in a small boat on a river. Sometimes the river runs slowly and gently, there are no alarms or excursions, and the boat just drifts along placidly. But sometimes there are rapids. The boat is tossed about, you are out of control, everything is happening fast, and all around there is tumult and confusion. Even if you know how to steer through the rapids, it isn't easy. If you don't know how, you panic, shout orders to each other, paddle desperately in different directions. In other words, I am suggesting that conflict is what happens when the boat of your relationship hits the rapids and you don't know how to steer through.

This analogy suggests a couple of helpful ideas. For one thing, while you are in the rapids it doesn't help to ask how you got there, or to try and allocate blame; the overwhelming priority is to get through in one piece. In fact, because the river is going there anyway and you are bound to hit some rapids sooner or later, it never makes much sense to blame your partner for the pickle you are in, tempting though it is. Like me, you can probably point, with tremendous conviction and righteousness, to exactly what it was that your partner said or did that has led you into the rapids, but it isn't particularly helpful or interesting. So I want to talk not about the content of any conflict, but about how to change the way you deal with it; how to get through the rapids without falling out of the boat.

The rapids are caused when the course of the river changes suddenly, when it narrows or drops a level; I think this is suggestive too. When your circumstances change markedly, the old agreements you made become irrelevant or inappropriate and old ways of doing things don't work any more. This allows the basic differences between the two of you – differences which agreement or habit kept under the surface – to pop up again. Suddenly, everything becomes a matter of principle, and matters of principle tend to be hard and unyielding. When two of them clash in opposition, sparks fly.

Increased intimacy is a bit like a change in the level of the river. After some time together partners can start to be much more open with each other; instead of keeping up appearances all the time as they do in the early stages of the relationship, they feel secure enough to admit failings and weaknesses to each other, even to ask for help. For some, physical intimacy takes on a whole new dimension once they have been with a partner long enough to be able to relax and be themselves sexually. They may decide to get married. All these changes seem to be good ones; ones which will lead the couple into greater closeness and love. That's certainly true in the long term. But what can be dreadfully puzzling and painful is that in the short term this kind of increased intimacy and commitment can lead to conflict. Again, it is not something one of them did or didn't do. It is the change in level that has created the entirely unexpected rapids they are going through.

In the face of conflict, the couple can make it worse. If they do, it is usually not deliberate; it's simply that they don't realize that the way they are behaving will have this effect. Unwittingly, they aggravate the differences between them and ignore what could unite them. These are, so to speak, basic errors in steering the boat, and they increase the risk that it will capsize and throw them out. Alternatively, the couple can learn to manage the conflict. They understand its nature and the way it affects them, and they take appropriate action to make sure that it doesn't become destructive. They have the knowledge and understanding which enables them to ride the rapids skilfully and safely, though they may feel nervous and tense as they go through. In fact, as will become clear by the end of the chapter, learning to manage the conflict does a lot more than merely keep it under control; it is the precursor to a lasting and creative enhancement of the relationship. Having successfully gone through the rapids together, the couple enters a new stage of life together, in a transformed relationship.

vicious circles

The first step in managing a conflict is to avoid making it worse. Imagine that a couple has two single electric blankets on their double bed. They hit on this arrangement because he always liked the blanket hotter than she did; this way they can each have the temperature that suits them. One day, by mistake the wires got plugged into the wrong blanket, so that his controls govern the temperature of her blanket, and vice versa. When he got into bed it was too cold for him, so he turned the dial up. Of course, the effect of that was to make her blanket hotter – so she turned down the control on her side. That made his blanket colder, so he turned the dial up more – and so on. What I'm getting at is that the actions that each of them takes makes the situation worse, not better. They are locked into a vicious circle.

Once a vicious circle gets established, then as soon as there is any conflict it will escalate. Perhaps the couple have got into a vicious circle over him not showing interest in her work – certainly, when they sit down for dinner he always talks about his work first, and when she tries to talk about hers his attention wanders, he interrupts, gets up to fetch another drink and doesn't follow up on what she's said. So she stops talking about her work, and starts to behave in the same way when he talks about his. Pretty soon, they don't discuss work at all. Then one day she makes a decision to change some aspect of her work and, in the habit now, doesn't tell him about it. When he finds out, he is annoyed. He accuses her of keeping it from him. She responds by saying that he never took an interest in her work anyway. You can imagine the rest. The consequences of the argument could be spread a lot wider than just talking about work; they might easily stop talking about all their hopes and plans and wishes, practically guaranteeing conflicts over those things in the future.

One way to break a vicious circle is for at least one person to stay at interface. For her, she would need not to get caught up with his apparent indifference to her work, would need not to respond in kind to his behaviour; in general, not to allow his energy to become hers too. Instead she would need to say what she wants to say, and perhaps even make sure that she talks first at dinner sometimes. If she was practised at staying at interface, she would have reported, much earlier, that she wanted him to pay attention to what she had to say. For him, assuming, perhaps charitably, that he didn't realize he wasn't listening properly, and even that he didn't think anything of it when she stopped talking about her work, he must have noticed when she started to interrupt him and wander off when he was talking. When he responded by not talking about his work he lost interface too and joined her in that energetic state of non-communication. It really is an energetic state; the air positively crackles with the tension of it, the host of unsaid thoughts which crowd round the table, continuously popping up and being rejected as unsayable. And, of course, he did it again, later, when he got annoyed with her; after all, she'd been annoyed with him for ages.

When people get caught in a vicious circle, they are each responding and reacting to the other, so they both slip easily into believing that the other person must change in order to stop it. But because it is a circle, either of them can break it at any time. It simply needs one of them not to react, but to stay at interface. Easier said than done, of course; when you're in it, it can take you over. Still, the key point for both partners is that waiting for the other to change ensures that they will both stay trapped in an escalating conflict.

resistance and the heart protector

What also makes a conflict worse is when one partner resists the other. Energetically, this is when one person won't allow the energy of his or her heart to synchronize with the other's. When your partner is doing this to you it feels as if you've just recognized an old friend in the street, your eyes meet, and he looks straight through you. It is confusing, upsetting and belittling. I'll explain in a moment the mechanism of this resistance, but first I want to add that it has another side to it. As well as not allowing the energy of his heart to come towards you, your partner doesn't allow your heart energy to touch him. It is as if you are reaching out a hand to him and he won't take it. Again, it feels awful.

In order to change this energetic resistance you have to understand its mechanism. In Chinese medicine the heart is considered to be supreme. It is the sovereign of all physical and mental processes, and takes responsibility for co-ordinating and harmonizing the activities of all the others. It is seen partly as an organ but more as a function which is located in the organ – in much the same way as we see the prime minister partly as a particular person but more as the holder of certain powers. Practitioners of Chinese medicine see the heart, in this wider sense, as crucial to a person's wellbeing. If it is injured, then everything else suffers. Most people have experienced a broken heart and know how devastating it can be; indeed, it is by no means fanciful to say that a person can die of a broken heart. So the heart has to be protected from injury.

Practitioners of Chinese medicine can distinguish an energetic process going on in the body which serves that function. It isn't known to Western medicine because that system of medicine understands the body as an assemblage of things, like cells or enzymes or muscles, and this is intangible. It is a highly specific movement of energy with a very particular purpose. One way of visualizing it is to imagine that there is a kind of Venetian blind around the heart. Turn the handle one way and the light streams through the horizontal slats; turn it the other and, as the slats become vertical, no light can get through. Or you can think of it as a net. If the net is expanded, then the holes open up and things can pass through. If the net contracts, the holes close up.

This energetic process, which from now on I'll call the 'heart protector',[2] closes up if there is anything coming towards the heart which could hurt it. When it is working well, it is extremely responsive and extremely accurate in its assessment of risk. That is, it recognizes the difference between words or actions which are benevolent and those which are not, distinguishing the helpful from the harmful. And it does so quickly enough to close up in the face of attack, and before its impact, and open out again in time to allow in affection and regard. It is not a deliberate process, there is no instruction from the brain to open and close the heart protector; it is an automatic, instinctive response.

But often it doesn't work well. Briefly, what goes wrong is that at some time or another it let in something which really hurt the heart. Perhaps, as in cases of abuse of a child by someone in a position of trust, the hurt was so overwhelming there was nothing it could do. Perhaps it was misled;

expecting a kind word from someone who loved us, it stayed open and received the blow of a cruel one. Whatever the cause, from then on it doesn't have its original natural and accurate responsiveness. There are many varieties of dysfunction of the heart protector – the one which is relevant here is that, having had this experience in the past, as soon as it senses any risk of a threat it closes up and stays closed.

If a person's heart protector is closed, then the energy of that person's heart cannot radiate out. Others will not feel warmth and affection coming from him; on the contrary, he will seem remote, cut off, unavailable – possibly even cold and calculating. What is more, whoever tries to re-establish loving contact by extending heart energy to him, including his partner, will make little impression. The overtures of affection will just bounce off the shell of his closed heart protector. It's tragic for both of them. She will feel rejected, and he will be starving to death inside that shell.

Before I go on to what can be done about it, I want to mention one important consequence of having a closed heart protector. As I mentioned in an earlier chapter, in normal circumstances the energy of the heart is far stronger than that of the other organs; next strongest, and a long way behind, is the energy of the brain. But if the heart protector is closed – and there is nothing else going on which would strongly activate the energy of one of the other organs – then the energy of the brain will be the one which will be felt by others. The contrast between the two of them is dramatic.

The energy of the heart is all-embracing. It identifies with what we all share, our common experiences of joy and pleasure, loss and suffering. It doesn't just feel for one person; it feels for others too. The films of famine in Ethiopia, shown on UK television on Red Nose day, prompted an enormous wave of charitable giving. As far as the heart is concerned, the people of Ethiopia are friends or neighbours; in a way they are ourselves. The heart doesn't distinguish or draw boundaries between people, it just responds to them. The brain on the other hand is concerned with the individuality of each person and works tirelessly to protect it. My brain identifies with me and thinks about how to make me happy, comfortable and safe – never mind anyone else. It takes out insurance and tells me to be careful. If I have any spare money it whispers to me that I should put it aside for a rainy day, whereas the heart wants me to give it away. It isn't that one energy is better and the other worse – we all have both just as we all have both arms and legs – but each has a different function, and it isn't the function of the brain to bring us close to others and embrace them; its function is to create and preserve our individuality. That's why I said earlier that a closed heart protector can make a person seem cold and calculating, and it is also why, in many conflicts between couples, all the talking doesn't help. If it is carried on from the brain alone, it widens rather than bridges the gap between them.

So if a person's heart protector is closed, others who want to get close to him will feel a kind of barrier in the way. Whatever they say or do, they will get a response which points out differences rather than agreement and mutuality. Words or actions which express the energy of the brain will have that quality of emphasizing and reinforcing separateness. It's another vicious circle. The repression of the heart's energy allows dominance of the brain's energy; and the more that happens the more others will feel rejected and pushed away. In the face of this, they'll start to withdraw too. 'Ah ha!', says the brain. 'There you are. I told you that you needed to be separate, that you couldn't trust people, that they didn't really care for you; now look what's happening'; and it carries on keeping others at a distance. The brain, of course, doesn't point out that it is helping to create what it is complaining about.

If it is your partner's heart protector which is closed there is not a great deal you can do about it, I am sorry to say. Staying at interface helps, because it stops the vicious circle from gathering momentum; so does showing affection by gestures and actions rather than words – the brain is so good at interpreting words to mean what it thinks they mean that it can distort practically anything you say to justify its view of the situation. Trying to talk sensibly about what is happening, analysing how it has come to pass, is almost certainly doomed to failure; the brain is really adept at using that kind of reasoning to stay safely apart. It finds it harder to defend its position against a loving look, an outstretched hand – so use those instead. What you can do, and it is vital, is to be available to your partner when his or her heart protector starts to open again. It may happen in a moment or it may be a slow and cautious process – rather like a tortoise's head coming out of its shell. Whichever it is, what happens next depends on the reception it gets. If it is met with recriminations and blame, you can be sure it will close up again. If it is met by a welcome, and feels safe in spite of what the brain has been saying, then it will stay open and open more. It takes a good deal of generosity on your part to be welcoming to this person who has been resistant to you for hours, days, weeks, but that's what will maintain and amplify the change in your partner's energy.

If it is your heart protector which is closed, and you want the relationship to survive, you will have to take some step towards opening it again. The various forms of energy medicine can be of enormous help because they can boost the energy of the heart protector (see appendix one, page 128). Otherwise there are two basic approaches. One is to quieten the brain – its activity is partly what is keeping the vicious circle going. You can do this by getting absorbed in some activity which demands concentration rather than thinking; meditation is the obvious technique but stripping paint or gardening can do it just as well. But sooner or later that activity will come to an end and you'll be back with your thoughts. What works best, in the long term, is refusing to have the next thought.[3] I'll explain what I mean by this. Thinking often has a runaway quality to it; once you start on a train of thought, for example thinking of all the ways in which your partner has been wrong about something, each thought leads on to the next and the brain adds instance upon instance, grievance upon grievance, relentlessly. Even thoughts which seem constructive, which are about how the impasse between the two of you might be broken, will fuel the energy of the brain and the schemes and stratagems you come up with will get in the way of you starting to relate to your partner from the heart again. The brain can't resist the next thought almost like an alcoholic who can't resist the next drink. But the impulse to follow the train of thought, just like the alcoholic's impulse to follow one drink with the next, can be resisted. As soon as you notice the next thought arising – 'and that's because . . .' or 'I asked her over and over again to . . .' – you just don't allow yourself to go on with it. You turn your attention to something else; there are plenty of other things to think about.

The other basic approach is to create an environment in which the heart protector can relax and allow the heart's energy to flow again. Do things which gladden your heart. If it isn't easy to open your heart to your partner, open it to your children by playing with them, to the beauty of the countryside, to music which moves you, to places you knew and loved as a child, to knitting, to table tennis – whatever it is that makes you feel joyful. In a way it's a trick, but it is more than that. You are oiling the heart protector, so to speak. Once it has freed up, started to move again in one situation, it is easier for it to do it in another. The point is to restore its flexibility, its normal functioning, its responsiveness to the outside world. Of course it may close again when you are with your partner, but it is much less likely to stay firmly shut irrespective of what he or she says or does, and it will at least have the potential to open if affection is being offered. And the fact that it has opened, even if it is in another context, makes it more likely that affection will be offered. Your energy body will have changed through your experience of feeling joyful, and your partner will be able to pick up on that. There will be something to build on, some energy of love which can be amplified.

passive aggression

Passive aggression is anger which is repressed; that quiet, needling hostility which wears the face of patience and reasonableness. There are all sorts of plausible reasons for repressing anger – a fear of hurting the other, a fear that if it is expressed it will kill the relationship, memories of a childhood fear of angry parents. Clearly fear is at the basis of repression – I'll say more about this shortly – but the first step in dealing with repressed anger is to realize that you have it. If, like me, you have been really good at burying your anger, you'll go around saying that you don't get angry and that you never feel rage and fury. Maybe you don't, but if you have ever felt disappointed with someone, frustrated with her, regretful that she isn't different, resentful about something she has done, irritated by some habit or other, then the chances are that the energy of anger did rise up in you but was repressed. All the feelings I have listed are ways in which this energy leaks out from underneath the repression.

The energy of anger is tremendously forceful; it is an explosive movement upwards and outwards. So it takes an enormous amount of energy to keep it in; it's like keeping a lid on a pressure cooker. Using up all that energy just keeping the anger in means that a person will have much less available for the rest of life. He or she may feel chronically tired, may find it hard to cope with work and daily life. If routine tasks take all the available energy there will be none left for enjoying sunny days and time with friends. This can lead to depression; there is so little energy left to spare that the person becomes progressively more listless and uninterested in the outside world. It can lead to physical symptoms in the area of the body where the rising energy is held in. When energy is blocked and cannot flow it becomes toxic; pain is blocked energy.

To explain this toxicity, water provides the best analogy. When it flows fast it stays clean and wholesome but when it becomes stagnant it can be poisonous to drink. By analogy, if energy can flow and move a person through all the emotions, experiencing grief, fear, anger and so on when appropriate, then he or she will stay healthy and well. You can see this natural flow of emotion clearly in small children. They hurt themselves or get frightened, and a moment later, with tears still wet on their cheeks, they are playing and laughing again.

Hence the remedy for the blocked energy of anger is obvious; allow it to move. But don't jump to the conclusion that this means shouting at your partner, throwing plates or hitting pillows.[4] Taking the lid off the pressure cooker is dangerous. Hitting pillows seems innocuous enough, but I'm not so sure. It suggests to your brain and body that hitting helps; and that feeds the newly released energy until it dominates your energy body. You may feel calmly exhausted once you have finished hitting the pillow, but the energy hasn't changed; it's just taking a break from all that exertion. Repressed anger can be moved without being allowed to explode; it can be transformed without being acted out.

In thinking about moving or transforming this energy, remember that it is the energy of springtime. It is what bursts buds from wood, what pushes plants through cracks in concrete and powers the growth of climbing roses. In other words it is both immensely forceful and essentially creative. It needn't blow things up; it can allow them to expand and blossom. The natural direction for this energy to take, the way it flows easily and naturally, is to let it lift the spirits, bring a smile to the lips, come out in gladness of heart. In terms of emotion, anger transforms into joy. If you simply use it – for knocking down a wall, protesting against injustice or organizing some event – you may get a lot done but it won't change and it won't go away.

So to move it, do something which brings you joy. Preferably choose something which doesn't have an aim or a goal, because these will tend to keep the energy focused and prevent it from expanding outwards; and it is in the expansion that its force is dissipated and becomes warmth to self and others. You can do it with your partner, but if you are too angry to allow yourself to have joy with him, you can do it on your own. Go for a run, turn the music up and dance, go out and have a laugh with a group of friends – whatever does it for you. If it is your partner who is angry you can help him best by sweeping him off to something you know he loves: of course he will be grumpy and difficult and will probably resist. But if you can somehow carry on in spite of his obvious ill-will, it's the best thing you can do for him and for the relationship.

A reader commented that this seemed rather feeble. She couldn't believe that doing something she loved would make the slightest difference when she was angry with her partner. I asked her if she'd ever tried it. With commendable honesty, she said 'no'.

I really understand her reaction. As I said in the introduction, we have all been schooled in the belief that it must be difficult, that we must expose and painstakingly dissect the content of any dispute with our partner. So not only do we overlook other possibilities, we reject them out of hand when they are suggested. But passive aggression is a toxic energy. It is the energy of anger when it has become stuck. To get it moving again you have to channel it in the direction it will flow most easily and naturally, and that is towards warmth, openness and light-hearted joy.

There is another remedy too. I said earlier that fear was at the root of the repression of anger. It is fear which keeps the lid on it so that it builds up behind that barrier; so if you can find out what you are afraid of you can start to do something about it. There are many levels of fear. If you look deeply you may find it has its roots in childhood, with fear of a parent or sibling, fear of being hurt, abandoned, unloved. You may see that while these fears left a strong impression on you, they are no longer relevant or appropriate to the life you now have, and you may be able to stop seeing what your partner does in the same light. Certainly, the deeper you go, the greater the transformation. But for practical purposes, what it usually boils down to is fear that if you tell your partner the truth – the truth about something you did, about how hurt you were by his behaviour, about your thoughts – he will reject you and the relationship will be over.

This is a crisis point in any relationship. If you carry on not telling the truth about these things, the relationship may slowly wither away and may die. By withholding this information from your partner you are demarcating areas of yourself and your life which you are not willing to share. And they breed. The longer you go on doing this, the more you have to keep from your partner because what you have just done, what you have just thought, what you mind now, all has its roots in what you did or thought before. And once you open up, you have to be willing for all of it to come out – either you are open or you are not. It doesn't take long before that seems impossible; there is so much of it and, you argue to yourself, it seems so petty to bring up all that old stuff now. The risk is that if you don't it'll lead to repressed anger, to illness in later years and to a sclerotic relationship.

However, if you do open up and tell the truth there is that risk that you will be rejected and your partner will walk out. There is no way round that. It is indeed a risk. The only question is whether or not you are willing to take it. And the only useful thing I have to say about this very difficult crisis point is to remind you that the other route is not risk free either.

The two strategies for dealing with repressed anger both operate on the barrier which is keeping it blocked in the body. One is to dismantle the barrier by removing the fear which created it in the first place and which continues to reinforce it as the years go by. The other allows the energy out so it can flow naturally and engender creativity and joy.

overt anger and the container

I know it sounds odd, but some people are really good at being angry. They get angry quickly, they tell their partner clearly and simply what they want or what they refuse to accept, they don't tack hurtful criticism on to that message, and when they've said what they had to say they let it go. It is clean and straightforward. However, most people aren't good at it, and when either or both partners express anger it is often damaging for them individually and devastating to the relationship. Perhaps, slowly, people can get better at being angry and at accepting their partner's anger; but in the short term what helps most are some strategies for managing it. As ever, I am not concerned with the content of anger, the specific grievance, but with its energy.

Again, the basic idea is to transform this energy. Overt anger, however, isn't stuck; moving it isn't the problem. The problem is dealing with its force and destructive potential. The question, therefore, is how to transform an explosion. And the answer is to contain it.

To see what containing energy can do, it is easiest to start by thinking of physical containers.[5] The way charcoal was made in the old days was to select sticks of the right kind of wood and stack them, layer upon layer, into a dome. Then clods of earth were piled up over the dome, a blazing stick was pushed into the middle and the whole lot set alight. The charcoal burners had to tend the fire for some days. If they saw smoke escaping from a crack between the clods, they had to get more earth and stop it up. If they didn't, the fire would reduce the sticks to ash. If they could keep the fire contained, its intensity would turn the sticks to charcoal. Essentially, it is the same process which produces coal and diamonds. You can see the same principle at work in a car engine. A series of tiny explosions, when petrol and air are ignited in the carburettor, can turn the wheels because each one is contained within a very small cylinder; that's the container. If there is a crack in the metal of the cylinder, then energy escapes and the car won't move. By contrast, the whole point of a bomb is that the container isn't strong enough. The point is to allow the energy out so that it destroys everything around it. In general terms, then, transformation comes from containing energy rather than letting it dissipate into the environment.

Applying this to the energy of anger in relationships, the idea is to create a strong enough container so that instead of building a bomb, something which explodes when either or both of you is angry, you can build what chemists call a retort – something in which transformation can take place. I will come to the nature of that transformation shortly; first I want to describe the equivalent of the physical container. It is a set of strong understandings, agreements, practices, expectations and conventions which the couple share and which, taken together, hold in the energy of anger. In describing the set of understandings and so on which constitute a container, different people will have different priorities – what is most important for you may not be what is most important for me. But for all couples, the more of these understandings they share, the stronger will be the container they have built.

Commitment makes a huge difference. If either of you is in the relationship unless something better comes along, or providing your partner looks after you, or until the going gets tough, then an outburst of anger has less chance of transforming the way you relate to one another. Having this ready-made, pre-planned option to quit amounts to a crack in the wall of the container; energy can leak out and the possibility of change, forged in the intensity of the contained energy, will be lost. Instead of paying attention to the anger when it erupts, a calculation is being made – 'Would I rather deal with this or would I rather walk out?' Even if the person decides to stay, attention will be on that question and not on understanding the issue or appreciating what has made the other angry in the first place – for however short-fused the angry person, this energy always arises from some real pain, some genuine distress. To return to the image of a boat going through the rapids, it is as if one person is busy calculating whether or not this is the moment to jump out of the boat instead of concentrating on how to paddle it to get through. I'm not saying it is never right to leave a relationship, never right to break a commitment. All I'm trying to get at is that if the commitment isn't there, then anger is much more likely to be destructive and much less likely to lead to some beneficial change.

Sexual fidelity also provides a container. There are lots of reasons for this – many of them obvious. Energetically, the issue is that the intermingling of the energy bodies of a couple who are sexually faithful produces something which they alone share; it is, in a sense, their private world. If a partner has had sexual relations with someone outside the relationship, that private world, which is a kind of container, is broken. The couple create something unique when their energies meet sexually, a bit like the colour you get when you mix a bit of this paint and a bit of that together; add a third dollop of paint and you lose the colour you had. Specifically, the energy of the one who has been unfaithful will be different – his or her energy body will have taken on some of the vibration of the third person's energy body, and it will now feel strange, unfamiliar, uncomfortable to his or her partner. What is more, whether or not the couple resume sexual relations, in the close proximity of daily life that partner is bound to be affected by the new vibration.

This is difficult enough to deal with if that partner knows what has happened; at least then there is an explanation for the new and unwelcome feelings of discomfort. If the infidelity is concealed it is even harder; the partner will feel confused and uncertain about the reality of those feelings, and that will leave his or her energy body in a disorganized state. Added to this is the ironic phenomenon of the attitude of the deceitful, unfaithful partner. Tolstoy, describing Anna Karenina's attitude to her husband, immediately after her concealed adultery, speaks of her 'setting against him everything bad she could find in him and forgiving him nothing, on account of the terrible fault towards him of which she was guilty'.[6]

Regular daily life provides another kind of container. The home, the children, the mutual friends, the way you know what your partner likes, the shared history which comes out in private jokes and allusions. All these bind the couple together in an unseen web of interconnections. Changing circumstances can weaken this container. When one partner moves into a new social world that the other doesn't know, when work takes one of them away from home a lot, when the children finally leave – the energy of anger poses more of a threat at times like these.

safety and transformation

The outcome of all this is that if the couple can pay attention to the energy rather than the content of their conflicts, they can create the conditions under which their anger can be transformed into a more open, expressive and honest kind of communication than they have had before. With a safe environment, they can start to let go of old habits and inhibitions which block intimacy at the first sign of trouble. If you are on the receiving end of anger, a container makes it possible for you to pay attention to your partner. Without the fear that this is leading, sooner or later, to abandonment, you can actually listen to what is being said, to appreciate what is really going on for him or her. Once again, it is really a matter of staying at interface. Although no doubt criticism is being hurled at you, in an odd sort of a way you don't have to take it personally. With real attention, you can see that your partner has been hooked by something, has had some old wound rubbed, is reacting out of habit. Probably what you said or did has triggered it, and you may learn to be more skilful so that you can avoid triggering it in future; but triggering it is different from causing it. The causes are old and deep. Knowing all that and not disappearing into your own anxieties or closing your own heart protector will start to change your partner's energy. It won't be amplified by your reaction and it will be calmed by your attention. Once again, it is remarkable, but true, that paying real attention to any energy changes it.

For the one who feels that rising explosive energy, what happens is a shift from expressing hostile anger to a new and more real way of communicating and relating. It is more real partly because, with a strong container giving a sense of security and safety, it is possible to get beneath the anger and to know and communicate what is fuelling it. Usually that is the need to say 'no' and the fear of the consequences of saying 'no'. You can't show fear unless you feel very safe. And it is more real because how you are can be an original response to the particular person you are with rather than ingrained responses to the people you were with in the past. Before, when you couldn't admit the fear you had to shout. So too when you couldn't say 'no' simply and clearly, but had to make a tremendous fuss to justify it. Instead, 'True anger of the moment gives the self permission to say no.'[7] That 'no' can be said without violence or aggression; and if it is coupled with some recognition of your own fear, it can be said lovingly.

And the overall effect on the relationship is that the more each person can say 'no' without calling down the heavens to justify it, the more 'yes' means. It takes on a new dimension; it becomes not passive, mild assent, but a powerful and compelling assertion of truly being a couple.

chapter five

deepening love

Most of us, both men and women, are terrified of merging our hearts with another. We say we're not, but we are . . . At a certain point, once you've established your separate identity, it's imperative that you let yourself lose it again.

Marianne Williamson, *Enchanted Love*[1]

There is an old saying that opposites attract. Some people, when they fall in love, are aware that what they find attractive in the other is that oppositeness. He is attracted to her dynamism, gaiety and charisma; she is attracted to his quiet self-sufficiency, his diffident way and his dry sense of humour. The energy bodies of the partners tend to be opposites too – one is more intense, the other more relaxed; one is quicker, the other slower; one is quite orderly, the other a bit chaotic. Even if people aren't conscious of this when they fall in love, impressed as they are by how well they understand each other, they usually become aware of it later; particularly if their attitude towards it changes, as it tends to. Whereas he used to love her quickness he now starts to complain about the fact that she never sits still, never finds time to be together doing nothing much. She used to love his quiet calmness, but now wishes he took the initiative more, was willing just to walk out of the house without first collecting everything he might possibly need. Partners often have their first serious conflicts when each stops being intrigued and delighted at how different the other is and starts to become frustrated and aggravated by the other's unaccountable preferences and behaviours.

Over time, the way the couple deals with these differences is important. They may be allowed to harden into roles; that is, the partners may implicitly agree to divide up life between them and from then on they are careful that neither encroaches on the territory of the other. They allocate the outgoing, sociable, active role to one, and the quiet homemaker role to the other. He is designated the impulsive, creative one, so she has to take the role of being unimaginative and reliable. If they do this, life may well be comfortable and familiar but there are two possible drawbacks. One is that each partner may well neglect talents, abilities and impulses which fall in the other's territory. She may actually be very creative, or may discover a blossoming creativity later in life; if she suppresses it, because to allow it out would upset the agreed arrangement, that is a real loss. The other drawback is that taking on these kinds of roles may prevent the deepening of love between them.

That's because love deepens when a couple manages to make a particular change in the way they relate to each other, when they cross a particular barrier. In order to do that they have to be able to see each other in a new light, one not dominated by that perception of oppositeness which attracted them to each other in the first place and which can drive them into polarized roles. To explain the nature of that barrier, and the way it can be crossed, I need to explain another aspect of the energy body.

differences and unity

The energy body has a number of vortexes of energy, rather like whirlpools; they are usually called chakras. Six of them permeate the physical body at the places indicated on figure 3, and indeed extend beyond it; the seventh is largely outside the body. They have been known about, and used in Eastern medical and therapeutic practice, for literally thousands of years. Current biochemical research, coming from a completely different point of view, can see the same pattern.

> A bearded yogi turned up at my office one day to ask me if endorphins were concentrated along the spine in a way that corresponded to the Hindu chakras . . . I pulled out a diagram that depicted how there were two chains of nerve bundles located on either side of the spinal cord, each rich with the information-carrying peptides. He placed his own chakra map over my drawing and together we saw how the two systems overlapped.
>
> Candace Pert, *Molecules of Emotion*[2]

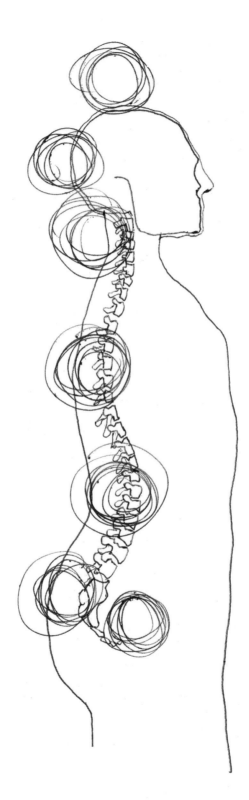

figure 3

Dr Fritz Smith, with the eye of a Western osteopath, saw the chakras from another perspective. Put simply, he pieced together a number of separate observations. The human body is a vertical structure, and the spine at its centre has many curves. Energy flows down vertical structures – think of lightning rods. And where energy flows around curves it creates an eddy or vortex. If you look at a stream where it flows round a bend you'll see lots of swirls in the water; there is usually a big one on the inside of the bend and lots of smaller ones where the flow hits particular obstructions. Hence, he realized, energy flowing down the spine will create eddies at the curves, at exactly the places where countless practitioners of meditation, Yoga, Tai Chi and so on have reported them to be.

What they have also reported is that the energy of each of these eddies or chakras has a particular quality to it. To be accurate, there is only one energy, but it takes on a particular quality in each chakra. Imagine that each chakra is glass of a different colour. The light that shines through each of them is the same, but they will all look different. So, the quality of sexual energy, for example, is different from that of maternal energy, and both of them are different from the kind of energy you use when you take a group of schoolchildren on an outing. The different energies enable us to do different things. Also there is a fundamental difference between the energies of the first three chakras and those of the remaining four. There is more on this later; for now, it is the first, or lower, three chakras which concern us. The box on page 88 sets out a very simple version of the qualities of energy in each of these chakras and the potentials they give us.[3]

When two people feel drawn towards one another they may be sensing differences between their energy bodies, and in particular in the state of the energies of these three chakras. If he has only weak energy in his first chakra, for example, he may be immensely attracted to a woman whose energy there is strong. Because of that she will be very stable, very grounded, and will feel comfortable with herself and in her body. To him, she will seem to offer a sense of security and safety which he doesn't feel himself. If she is also attracted to him, it may be because she likes to feel needed. But if the attraction is strong, there'll probably be another contrast between their energies too; perhaps he has very strong energy in his third chakra, where hers is weak. Hence, she will find his competence in the world offers reassurance and protection to her in an area of life where she feels vulnerable. And, reciprocally, he enjoys feeling needed in that way. Each recognizes that the other can provide support in an area of weakness, and each enjoys the feelings of self-worth that come through giving that support.

THE LOWER THREE CHAKRAS

QUALITY OF ENERGY	POTENTIALS
FIRST CHAKRA Supporting, nurturing, containing, belonging; like being a child held by a mother	Feeling secure in the world. A sense of being at home with yourself and in your body
SECOND CHAKRA Dynamic, creative, outgoing, erotic; like being a dancer, carried away by the music	Sexuality; starting new projects, making things happen, new phases of life
THIRD CHAKRA Individualistic, forceful, organizing; like being the captain of a ship	Willpower, control, power, self-image; instrumental relations with others

It is easy to see how, in a long-term relationship, these partners could become very dependent on each other. It comes from sharing their energies in the way they might share ownership of a house or responsibilities towards aged parents. Given that her first chakra energy is so strong she has plenty to give him, so he doesn't bother to develop his own. Imagine that he works hard and has been successful in building up his own small business, but he does worry a lot. One of the reasons he works so hard is that he feels that the business is under constant threat; if it isn't cash flow problems it is the competition of rivals that makes him anxious. His accountant tells him that he needn't get so worked up – the company is financially secure and has plenty of goodwill – but he can't help it. In addition, although he is generally well liked, he has a reputation for being a bully. He knows that he can fly off the handle with subordinates whom he thinks are criticizing his decisions, even though, rationally, he realizes that what they have to say might be true and useful. With a different partner he might have to face up to the feelings of personal insecurity which lie behind his anxiety and his bullying. But with a partner who always manages to prop him up, so to speak, and who gives him enough of a sense that he is safe and secure, enough of a sense that it'll all be all right, he doesn't have to. The same kind of dynamic, with roles reversed, may be operating around the energy of the third chakra.

Something like this kind of mutual support happens in most relationships, and it can yield a good deal of affection, gratitude and respect on both sides; nothing wrong with that. But it is interesting to look at what it can do to the energy of each partner, and the energy of the relationship, over time.

The key point is that the differences between them constitute a kind of glue which sticks the two of them together in relationship. As the glue sets, the weaknesses of each partner are held in place. Where, initially, he didn't have to go to the trouble of developing the energy of his first chakra, after a time he won't be able to, even if he wants to, without threatening the bonds between them. His own energy cannot get stronger and thereby give him more potential as an individual without undermining the relationship itself. What was a liberation may become a prison. For both of them, change becomes threatening, and particularly change which makes either of them more rounded, more whole and more competent. It is a strange and ironic consequence of what started out as a gift and a joy. It is another instance of energy which is stuck becoming toxic.

As for the relationship, it will start to miss something wonderful. When the couple fell in love, each partner perceived the other in two apparently contradictory ways simultaneously. As I have said, each relished the differences between them, and appreciated the support of the partner's stronger energy just where each felt vulnerable. And at the same time, there was the experience of unity. Each felt they had found someone who was, in some mysterious way, the same. It was deeper than sharing the same interests or attitudes. They each felt that the other understood the hopes and the dreams, the pains and the confusions, in a way that no one else did. Sexually too, there can be the experience that the other is oneself in a different body. And all that seems to come not from discussing or explaining these things, but from some common shared core of their being.

Logic would say that the partner couldn't be both different and the same at once; a thing cannot be black and white at the same time. But logic may not be a good guide in the area of feelings, emotions and human experience. I think that it is possible to notice difference and unity at the same time; indeed, I think it is a key feature of love. Joseph Campbell once explained this with a brilliant analogy. He was in a lecture theatre when he was asked how he could say that each human being was both unique and the same as every other. He pointed up at the lights shining down at him on stage and said something like, 'There are lots of light bulbs, and each of them is separate. But the light that shines through them is the same.'[4] A crucial part of falling in love is noticing the light. A crucial danger of a relationship which has become dependent on the differences between the partners is that it has stopped noticing the light, and sees only light bulbs.

The energy of the first three chakras gives the power to notice light bulbs. All the business of normal life, carried on together over the years, feeds the energy of the first three chakras so that increasingly the partners see each other as different and not the same. It can become a vicious circle of the kind I described in the last chapter. The more that the couple build a shared life – children, house, car, insurance, shopping, family events, holidays – the more each depends on the differences between them to manage it. And the more that happens the stronger the differences become. Less attention is paid to that sense that the couple are one and the same. Accordingly that energy withers; as ever, 'energy responds to us'.

By contrast, the energy of the upper four chakras, and particularly the heart chakra, gives the power to notice light. I want to suggest that a relationship which grows and deepens over the years is one in which the energy of the upper four chakras stays at least as strong as the energy in the lower three. In a moment I'll come to how that can be done, but first I need to describe these chakras (see the box, right).

Just in case it isn't clear from these brief descriptions, I want to emphasize that the energy of each of these chakras enables a perception of unity, of what is common to all human beings. So, for example, the fifth chakra is the energy of truth, and ultimately truth doesn't depend on your character or personality, whether you are male or female, or what culture or even century you were born into. Of course, the world looks different to a person born male in the seventeenth century and one born female in the twentieth, and snorkelling may be delightful to one but terrifying to another. But the deeper truth of what I can only describe as 'how it is' is the same for all. This is the truth that science seeks and which saints and mystics of all ages, allowing for differences of language and context, all report in the same way. Similarly, the love and compassion engendered by the energy of the fourth chakra doesn't turn on only when your partner cooks you nice meals or does your laundry; nor does it turn off when she is preoccupied with her own problems and ignores you and your needs. It is love of a deeper level of humanness. It is the love of the universal life in that one particular person; the person is loved as an exquisite and unique manifestation of that universal life. When you have the delightful experience of seeing your

THE UPPER FOUR CHAKRAS

QUALITY OF ENERGY	POTENTIALS
FOURTH CHAKRA Compassion, loving-kindness, empathy; like Mother Teresa or the Dalai Lama	Serving and caring for others. A sense of oneness with others and the natural world
FIFTH CHAKRA Direct, clear, firm, open; like composing or hearing a great piece of music	Speaking the truth and hearing the real meaning behind the words
SIXTH CHAKRA Penetrating, visionary, comprehending and comprehensive; like looking through a powerful telescope or microscope	Perceptiveness, discrimination, a sense of purpose or mission in life
SEVENTH CHAKRA Pristine, refined, uplifting; like a sunny spring day after hours of rain	Awareness of other realms of reality and of consciousness; spirituality

partner as the same as yourself, it is a sign that this energy has been awakened.

In what follows I am going to concentrate on the fourth, or heart, chakra. When the energy of this chakra is activated it deepens the love between a couple. That's partly because this kind of energy gives access to a widely generous, tolerant and warm way of relating to each other. It makes no demands on a partner, and doesn't require him or her to compensate for your own weaknesses. Out of the window go all the conditions like, 'I'll love you if you stay the same' or, when the mind is in charge, 'I'll love you if you pretend I am who I think I am (and in return I'll pretend you are who you think you are).'[5] Out of the window go all those judgments about your partner's clothes, cooking, time-keeping, even his darker side (we all have one). Out of the window too goes that business of making comparisons, comparing your partner with who she used to be, could be, or might have been, or would be if she really loved you, and comparisons with others who, apparently, have all the talents, skills and qualities she doesn't have. Instead there is appreciation, acceptance, love. It is bliss both to give and to receive; to be touched by that energy.

It isn't too good to be true. It does happen, and a couple can learn to access and activate that energy more and more often. But it is too good to last. Fortunately, that doesn't matter. The point is not to spend the whole of one's time relating in this way, but to be able to move in and out of relating through differences and relating through unity. They are two sides of the coin of being human; one isn't better than the other or more important. Both of them are sources of joy and companionship and closeness. It is just that you don't want to cut yourselves off from half of what is available, from half of the love you can enjoy together.

Being able to relate through the energies of the higher chakras changes the meaning of relationship through difference. If a couple can only relate from the first three chakras, then, as I explained above, there is pressure on each partner to stick to his or her role. But having had the experience of relating through unity, and knowing that there are other ways to relate to each other, they can treat these roles lightly, taking them on and off as an actor does. You can imagine one asking the other over breakfast, 'Who do you want to be today?' Mulling it over, she answers, 'I think I'll be the spontaneous, impulsive, creative one.' If there are children to be looked after, for example, he might reply, 'Well, in that case I'll be the reliable, responsible one.' If, on the other hand, they are on their own, with no responsibilities, he might reply, 'I'll be that too,' and off they go with not a care in the world. In other words, the differences become a dance, a game; they don't have to take them too seriously. Knowing they aren't the only reality makes all the difference.

crossing the barrier

The energies of the lower chakras provide the impetus for individuation: becoming separate from the mother, the family, the society you grew up in, the conventions of that society and so on. They are also drawn on and valued, in Western society at any rate, through the whole business of getting on in the world, getting ahead, becoming special or important. Most of us have focused so intently on doing that, that we don't find it easy to shift our focus to the energies of unity, to an appreciation of our identity with others. In addition, there is a qualitative change involved which makes this hard to do. In the East, it is seen as a process of deliberately moving energy from the third to the fourth chakra, and it is regarded as a difficult and serious undertaking. In the body, these two chakras lie either side of the diaphragm, a thick strong band of muscle which divides the trunk in two just below the rib cage; moving energy up to the fourth chakra involves a crossing of this substantial barrier. This crossing is only attempted in the East after a long period of training and the guidance of a skilled teacher.

However, the force of romantic love is so strong that it can, and usually does, impel a person's energy across that barrier. That accounts for much of the change in the energy body when a person falls in love. Once that initial force has died down, as it will, the energy body will return to normal. For the couple that will probably mean that from then on they'll relate to each other mainly through the energies of the lower three chakras. But if the couple can find ways to cross that barrier and activate the energy of the upper chakras, they can also experience the kind of love they encountered in the early days, but this time with the added richness that it is set against the background of all they have shared and been through since. When I talk about activating the upper chakras, what I have in mind is not deliberately moving energy to the upper chakras – that requires a disciplined practice which is well outside the scope of this book – but creating the optimum conditions for it to happen.

You can best create those conditions by putting your attention on the energy of your own heart chakra. It is always there, though it may be dormant, and it will always embrace your partner, however unlikely this may seem when you are in the midst of some argument or dispute. In any day there will probably be at least one moment when, involuntarily, you feel the warmth of shared understanding. It might be as apparently trivial as laughing at the same joke on a TV programme or both relishing the feeling of clean sheets on the bed. Notice it; that's the energy you want to amplify through your attention. Comment on it to your partner; that will give her the opportunity of noticing it in herself, further amplifying that energy. If, to take another example, she tells you about something that happened during the day which she enjoyed or found upsetting, don't immediately start to think about how you would have reacted in those circumstances, which might well have been differently, but put yourself in her shoes and see if you can share in her emotion. Be aware of those fleeting impulses to do something kind or affectionate for her, which are called the 'promptings of love', and act on them. At all or any of these moments it may well be that you will hear an inner voice telling you to hold your ground, to maintain the distance between you, usually in order to justify the position you took some time ago. That will be a tiny crisis point at which you choose whether to go on or go back and at which your energy can move to the heart or stay where it is.

You can develop habits which will help; they may feel like tricks to begin with but as you become more accustomed to them they will feel quite natural. One is to look at your partner's eyes when she is talking. That's where you have the best chance of seeing what you have in common, at recognizing whatever it is that lies behind differences of personality or gender. The old saying 'The eyes are the windows of the soul' makes the point. And the more you keep looking through that window, the more you will encourage that aspect of your partner to reveal itself.

There's another habit which is useful in any serious conversation, especially if you start to argue. When you reply to what she has said, start by telling her what you agree with in what she has just said. So often we do the opposite. Listening to a partner, we seize on what we dispute or want to contradict, and as soon as she has finished we slap our refutation down like a winning ace in a card game. That feeds and amplifies the energy of difference; by contrast, starting with agreement feeds the energy of unity. And developing the habit of stating agreement will alter each of your own energies. As you are listening, you will be looking for what you agree with, in order to have something to say when she finishes. That will affect what you notice. You may spot something she says which you would otherwise have overlooked, you may hear between the lines, so to speak, and pick up a shared anxiety about the disagreement, or a shared willingness not to repeat the mistakes which led you into it. Your body language will change too in response to the change in your orientation – it will be less closed and more open. You may find yourself instinctively uncrossing your arms or legs and leaning forward in your chair.

Doing this will alter your partner's energy too. If, immediately after she's finished speaking, she gets hit by words of denial and criticism, she's bound to stiffen and become defensive. Her heart protector will close, and the chances are she won't really hear what you're saying. On the other hand, if that first response she gets is affirming, and carries a message of respect, then the chances are she will relax, open her heart protector a little more and start to repay the compliment.

What often happens then is that the conversation drops to a deeper level. Instead of picking up on each other's precise words, like lawyers scanning a contract, you both start to pick up on the level of the feelings that your partner is trying to express and wants you to appreciate and accept. In a sense, whether or not the two of you agree about the issue in question loses its importance. What comes to matter more, for example, is that she acknowledges that he is distressed, upset, anxious – whatever words convey emotional unhappiness and pain to you – and the fact that she might not have had those feelings in those same circumstances becomes irrelevant. Her acknowledgment comes from knowing what it is like to feel that because she's felt like that too. Again, that's emphasizing unity not difference.

When you touch him, to take another example, you might normally notice how different his body is from yours. Alternatively, you can get into the habit of sensing similarity. You have different energy bodies, but you both have energy. As you touch, be aware that he is alive, as you are, and see what that feels like. It sounds trivial, but in my experience, if you hug your partner concentrating only on the fact that he or she is alive it is quite different from a normal hug. It is extraordinary how vibrant it feels. And, as I explained in chapter two, you can use touch quite deliberately to bring the vibrations of your two energy bodies into harmony.

It helps to put your attention on fourth chakra energy in your partner. You can, if you choose, concentrate on the fact that he isn't tidy or punctual. No doubt these things are annoying, but how much attention are you going to give them? You can erect, on such things, an elaborate and watertight structure, of which each brick is a reason why the relationship is impossible. If you do, you won't have much energy left for noticing and appreciating what you share. It may seem as if you can't do anything about your reactions to your partner's behaviour, but you really do have a choice. Imagine you are rather delicate and precise and the fact that your partner is clumsy aggravates you. One day, when you are distressed, he comes and puts his arms round you in a rather clumsy way; it is up to you whether you pay more attention to the clumsiness or to the empathy.

Telling your partner the truth makes a huge difference too. Most people lie, or conceal, because they are frightened. A person may fear criticism or condemnation, fear being abandoned and rejected if his partner were to know what he thinks or what he's done, fear that he will lose his job, his promotion, the respect of his colleagues. At root, all these amount to a fear that if he tells the truth he won't survive. In a way that's true. He won't die, but the impression of himself he has given to others, and perhaps persuaded himself to believe too, will indeed die; it won't be able to survive the contrast with reality. The point is that lying is about protecting and preserving some self-image which makes a person different or special. Therefore it is using the energy of one or more of the lower three chakras. And it uses a lot of it; I know that when I have told a lie, and have had to maintain it resolutely, it has gobbled up energy. So if you don't tell your partner the truth you can't expect the energy of the higher chakras to get much of a look in. There's no spare energy, for one thing; and, for another, that's not where you are putting your attention.

Less obviously, being willing to hear the truth is important too. Your partner may be willing to open up to you, given the slightest encouragement, but you may be busy communicating, in a thousand tiny ways, that you don't want to know. You may say so straight out. Of course, you fear the worst, and even if it isn't as bad as that, it'll probably be uncomfortable or painful. But if you choose not to listen, you will be cutting yourself off from the energy of unity. The reason for this is that at that deeper level where you are the same, it must be the case that you have the potential to do whatever it is your partner has done. If that seems unimaginable and shocking, remember that those who have the most cause to condemn others, like Nelson Mandela, often seem to be the most forgiving. Perhaps that's because they recognize that the enemy is not so very different from themselves.

Being unwilling to hear the truth about yourself has the same effect as being unwilling to hear the truth about your partner. However, you have to be a bit careful about what you accept as the truth; people say all sorts of things to each other, especially in anger, and you don't have to assume that any criticism is true. Still, if you are so busy maintaining your own self-image that you cannot hear that you have been careless of your partner's feelings, or unkind, then you won't be open to the fact that she might love you all the same. Insisting on the fact that you weren't unkind, or insisting that you were right to behave as you did even if it seemed unkind, you will overlook the love. You might even persuade yourself that you can only be loved if you deserve it and if you are good; and that will take you a long way away from energy of the fourth chakra.

Finally, there is one more thing you can do. It is to be open to being surprised. Your heart chakra can kick in when you least expect it, and at the oddest and most inconvenient times. The most inconvenient time is when you are full of righteous indignation about what he has done, when you are determined to get him to accept that you are right about something and he is wrong. Or when you are in despair about the relationship, believing it serves neither of you. When, in other words, you are obsessed with what separates you. Normally, nothing happens to change that state. But occasionally, like an act of grace, something does happen. It might be a word or gesture from your partner, a glimpse of the delicacy of the hair on the nape of her neck, a strange sensation that there is a rightness about being together; whatever it is, it catches you and moves you to a new place. It evokes feelings of compassion, understanding and love. You can dismiss or ignore these feelings and return to the indignation and despair. Or you can, in C.S. Lewis's wonderful phrase, be willing to be 'surprised by joy'.

the heart again

I have talked about the energy of the heart in three ways in the last three chapters. I started with the idea that synchronizing the rhythms of the heart generates intimacy. In the next chapter I introduced the idea of the heart protector, and said that the extent to which you can give or receive love depends on how open or closed it is to your partner. Finally, in this chapter, I have suggested that activating the energy of the heart chakra leads to a deepening of the love between two people. You may be wondering how these three ideas fit together; is there a difference, for example, between synchronizing heart rhythms and activating the heart chakra; or are they the same? I'm afraid I don't know the answer to that question. I don't have a neat theory about the energy of the heart, one which incorporates all these ideas tidily. The ideas come from different sources and traditions, and I have picked them, like a magpie, because they fascinate me. Also, I have found each of them useful at one time or another. Actually, more than useful. They have shown me where and how I block out love from my life, and they have given me hope that I can learn to stop doing that. They have provided me with some simple practical rules of thumb: getting quiet, doing things which bring me joy, paying attention to what I share with my partner, looking at her eyes when she speaks to me. These may seem rather passive; they don't seem to be directed to making things happen. I think that's because, in the end, it isn't a matter of trying to create love or grow it or deepen it; wilful heroic activity misses the point. It is a matter of quietly, persistently, removing the blocks to love. The love is always there.

chapter six

times of change

Do not be afraid of what you are becoming.

Jamake Highwater, quoted in *The Hero's Journey*[1]

There is an underlying quality to each person's energy body which stays constant over time. My ninety-year-old father has a way of being in the world which you can see clearly in the family photograph taken when he was a six-year-old boy. Through both his relative inactivity now, and the forced stillness he adopted for the photograph all those years ago, shines the same quality of energy. It has a buoyancy, a vivacity and a certain restlessness which are all his own. Whatever the ups and downs of his life – periods of hard work or play, anxiety or grief – it has been a constant. Like the key in which a piece of music is written, it is the structure to which it is bound and the essential harmony to which it always returns. Your energy body is similarly unique and unchanging.

At a more superficial level, your energy body changes as you are affected by and respond to the events that life brings along. Two examples I have already mentioned are the changes which take place when you fall in love or get angry. These, to return to the musical analogy, are the changes of tempo, volume and orchestration, even temporary changes of key. Added to these are the changes which take place through the process of ageing. In old age, for example:

> I am now looking back and I can tell you that there's a wonderful moment when you realize, 'I'm not striving for anything.' What I'm doing now is not a means of achieving something later. After a certain

age, there's not a future, and suddenly the present becomes rich and it becomes a thing in itself which you are now experiencing.

Joseph Campbell, *This Business of the Gods*[2]

The short-term fluctuations in the energy body and the slower changes which come with ageing have one thing in common; they are not under your voluntary control. If you have had a shock, your energy scatters and you can't stop it happening. Similarly, if you feel anxious, it's no earthly use anyone telling you, or you telling yourself, not to feel that way. Of course you can be more or less skilful in the way you deal with these states, and if you know what to do about them you can recover more quickly. But you can't will them not to happen. The same is true of the changes in the energy body which come as part of the phases of life; energetically, being fifty is different from being thirty even if you are still as physically fit and active as you were.

When your partner's energy body changes, that will have an effect on you. It is all too easy to take this personally, to think that the change is some kind of attack. For one thing, change is usually threatening and when you are under threat it is quite natural to look around to find out where it is coming from, and quite natural to look first at your partner. For another, so much of what your partner says and does in daily life is directed at you that it is easy to jump to the conclusion that it is all directed at you. But given that changes in the energy body are not under your partner's control, this makes no sense. It is just what is happening to him or her, like going bald or the menopause. There are sensible things your partner can do about what has happened, and sensible things you can do to help – there's more on that later – but the most helpful thing you can both do is to understand that it is an involuntary energetic change.

At times of major change, like the birth of a first child, a financial crisis or retirement, there will be big changes in the energy bodies of both partners and hence a significant change in the energy between them. At these times the couple will have a lot on their plate dealing with a new and sometimes difficult situation, and thinking about what's going on energetically might seem a pretty low priority. But it doesn't take long to get a basic understanding of what is likely to happen and that can cut out a lot of unnecessary worrying. If you didn't know about the seasons, then you'd get really alarmed in the autumn as plants died, and get even more alarmed as autumn turned into winter. Knowing that spring will come makes all the difference. Once you realize that an energy has changed, that it was entirely natural that it should do so, and you understand the nature of the change, then you don't panic when it does and you have a pretty good idea of what to do in order to adjust to it.

peak experiences

Occasionally and irregularly we live through a particularly intense time and it has a powerful effect on us. These peak experiences can come about in a number of ways and last anything from a few moments to a few days. There is quite a wide range of them. At the mild end of the spectrum I remember a perfect day with my partner. The sun shone, the birds sang, the spring countryside was full of blossom, we found a wonderful place to swim and it was all rather magical – you know the kind of thing. Somewhere near the middle of the spectrum were times I spent on two courses where the intensity came from my excitement at learning something which seemed to me very new and immensely important and from the atmosphere which built up in the group as we worked together towards a common aim. And, as the days went by and trust built up between us, we each revealed a little more of ourselves to the others, so that by the end I felt immensely fond of all the participants – even those I hadn't much liked at the beginning. As the layers of self-image were discarded and people stopped trying to impress, charm or conceal, what was revealed was immensely lovable. I came home in a different state, and for a while I was more open and loving to those around me. It wore off, of course, but at the time it improved all my relationships. A rather different example, but also a time which had a marked effect, was a period of serious illness. As I lay in bed hallucinating from my high fever, something shifted in me and again, for a time, I was different afterwards.

At the extreme end of the spectrum are times of great crisis or danger. There are plenty of reports of mothers who lift cars or huge pieces of fallen masonry if their child has been pinned under them, using a strength they didn't know they had and wouldn't have at any other time. In the moment they have the capabilities which practitioners of martial arts spend years developing in order to be able to perform such feats at will. With total concentration and attention comes a dramatic change in the energy body, one which vastly increases the potential of the physical body. The energy body expands, it becomes highly organized and it vibrates more quickly. People often say, of these moments, that time seemed to slow down; perhaps that's the effect of the faster vibration which allows more perceptions and reactions in a given period of time than are normally possible.

It is natural and inevitable that after times like these the energy body will relapse back into its normal state. After an expansion comes contraction; it is the rhythm of life. After the expansion of the heart with blood, or the lungs with air, comes a contraction. After the flood tide comes the ebb. The same is true in relationships – although we often forget it and get upset when it happens. If you and your partner have had a wonderful time together, felt closer than ever before, experienced great sexual pleasure, you are shocked when you find that you are distant, even irritated with each other, the next day. You think there is something wrong, or you start to believe that you were kidding yourself about how wonderful it was, or you wonder if your partner was just putting it on. It's much more likely to be this basic dynamic of energy.

As your energy body contracts, you may feel it as sadness and loss. If the contraction is strong you may well experience it as embarrassment and self-consciousness. It's a shrinking feeling. It's as if you are remembering how you got roaring drunk the night before and danced semi-naked on the dinner table, scattering plates and glasses with utter abandon. You want to crawl into a burrow and hide and not see the people who witnessed it ever again. If the embarrassment is severe you may experience it as shame. It's a corrosive emotion. It eats away at you and attacks you at a deep level. If it lodges there it can have a considerable influence on how you respond in the future, especially to situations of great intimacy and openness. It may make you pull back from them and try to break the tension they evoke in you with a joke or a gesture which distances you from your partner. On the other hand, if you can remember that what you are feeling is not a rational reaction to having made a mistake but just the experience of your energy body contracting, as it must, then the embarrassment or shame won't lodge in the body and won't inhibit your natural instinct to relish the good times.

hard times

Many couples go through a time when, although there is no conflict between them, things are difficult; they have run up a debt and don't know how to repay it, a child is seriously ill and it is not clear what to do for the best, they are both under stress at work and can't see a way of reducing or resolving it. Every couple's circumstances, every couple's difficulties are individual, but there are two things worth knowing which can help a couple to get through.

At these times there will often be hard decisions to be made, and hard decisions take a lot of energy. Each person will be working with partial information, trying to weigh up a complex set of factors and assessing apparently incompatible options. There may well be moral dilemmas involved too. All this is demanding enough, but it can be even tougher when the couple try to reach a joint decision. That's partly because they'll probably have to negotiate some kind of agreement which reconciles their different points of view. And it is partly because when the pressure is on, people tend to revert to childhood patterns of behaviour, which generally don't help at all and add another layer of complexity to the couple's discussions. Of course, the two of them have to embark on all this when things are difficult anyway, and what they really want to do is take a break from it all.

Making a hard decision takes energy like running a marathon takes energy. Just acknowledging that will help. You wouldn't dream of running a marathon without doing some training – so you take smaller decisions first, by way of practising. Nor would you dream of running a marathon just before going to bed; so you make sure you tackle the decision when you're not tired and when you have enough time to do it properly. And you will realize that when you've taken it you might well be exhausted. You may feel it straight away or it might not hit you until quite a lot later, a delayed reaction. But you won't be hard on yourself, or your partner, when either of you spends a day in bed, or flopped on the sofa watching TV. You will need to recover from the effort, however you each do that.

Another feature of difficult times is that there isn't enough of something. Often it's money, but it can be space or time. We all know about not enough money and not enough time, but lack of space can be very hard. The couple may live in a cramped house, or without a garden, or with too many people for the room they have. The walls are thin and there is no real privacy. Living on a busy street can give the feeling that there isn't enough; there is nowhere outside to sit, nowhere to put things you want to get rid of, and the traffic noise invades every room. It can be powerfully oppressive if the buildings are close together, and you look out of your windows on to a blank wall or into another person's living room.

It is odd and interesting that energy registers abundance and deprivation, but it doesn't register what the abundance or deprivation is about. It is just expansion or contraction. You can experience plenty from having a wonderful hour with your partner, however, tight your circumstances, just as a tax exile may be sitting in his holiday home in the sun feeling utterly bereft. Energetically, space, time and, to some extent, money, are interchangeable.

So if you haven't got enough space, and you can't find a way of getting more, then you change that rather depressing cramped energy by making more time. Make sure, quite deliberately, that you have masses of time for the things you like doing. Prepare meals carefully and linger over eating them together; go to the shops you really like, never mind that they are an hour or two away, and potter round them to your heart's content. Paint a room absolutely meticulously, create a family photograph album with loving care. Energetically, really taking your time over activities you like doing will feel like abundance and that will make it much easier to live in a cramped space. Similarly, if you are both so busy that there's never enough time, you can change that rather frantic energy by making more space. Try and get an office with a view from the window, and make sure it is uncluttered. When you are at home together, use the biggest room in the house, and make it really simple and elegant. Spend as much time as you can out of doors. When you have holidays, don't visit cities but go to the sea, the mountains, the desert.

Not having enough money is a bit trickier because it tends to go with one or both of the others. Still, with a little ingenuity there may be room for manoeuvre. J.K. Rowling was very short of money when she wrote the first Harry Potter book, and she lived in Edinburgh where heating is both essential and expensive. So she wrote in a café, creating more space at the same time as saving money. Getting up half an hour earlier is always possible, and so is getting organized so that you do things more efficiently.

The thing to avoid is deprivation in all three together; that really contracts the energy body, and the energy of the relationship too. For the vast majority of people, it is actually quite easy to avoid. There are some who get into deprivation carelessly – they just can't be bothered to manage their money, get things organized sensibly or clear the junk out of the front room. There are others who take it on as a kind of hair shirt; they don't feel they deserve abundance so they deliberately, if unconsciously, make sure they don't have enough. I'm not suggesting that these habits are easy to change. But for anyone who is likely to be reading this book, there will be one of the three which really can be expanded.

the mid-life crisis

Energy is unstable, volatile and sometimes chaotic when it changes direction. And at some time, usually in your forties, your energy starts to change direction. Up until then it has been predominantly directed outwards; now it begins to turn inwards. In your twenties and thirties your energy is focused on the world outside – a partner to be found, children to be cared for, a career to be built, a home to be created. It is as if your energy is a torch which you shine out on what interests and concerns you.[3] In your forties, quite involuntarily, you find that you've started to turn your torch on yourself. The force of this change of direction is different for each of us, and each of us experiences it and reacts to it differently; but it is as much a part of a human lifetime as the spots of puberty or the wrinkled skin of old age.

What you notice, what you see as if for the first time in the light of the torch, is that you're not so sure any more who you are. Things which you assumed were settled, assumptions you've held for years, may begin to feel rather pointless or unimportant. It can be very unsettling. Your attitudes and beliefs about yourself, about what you like and want, which have seemed so obvious and straightforward for years, now look a bit shaky or just plain wrong. For many women it coincides with the menopause, which brings its own pressures to re-evaluate. I remember a friend telling me what a profound change it was for her when, in public places, men she didn't know no longer took a good look at her; instead their eyes slid past. Although she had never particularly liked that kind of attention, it felt like a loss not to have it any more. She realized how much of who she thought she was had been bound up with that instinctive reaction she had drawn from men.

For many men, this energetic shift coincides with a dawning realization that all the things they thought they might do one day may no longer be possible and that their physical strength isn't what it was either. In some men this sparks a denial. They buy a sports car or take up with a much younger woman. In others it pushes them to abandon a career and take up the work they always wanted to do. If, as is often the case, this energetic change in both men and women starts at roughly the same time as their children begin to become sexual beings, begin the teenage rejection of the family way of doing things, and soon afterwards leave home, then the couple is faced with a lot of adjusting. It isn't surprising that many relationships run into difficulties at this time.

To see how such changes might be managed, and how they can be incorporated into the relationship instead of pulling it apart, I need to say a bit more about what is happening energetically.

There is an aspect of the chakras which I didn't mention in the last chapter but which is relevant here. Although all the seven different qualities of energy of the chakras are operating all the time in all of us, each chakra has a particular charge, an extra force or dimension to it, at each stage of life. Starting at the base chakra, the higher ones are activated and emphasized in turn, almost like lights being switched on by the energy as it rises. At some time in a person's forties, the throat or fifth chakra gets switched on. The energy here is both refined and ruthless. It discriminates what is really true from what is not, and puts energy behind the truth. So it becomes much more difficult to go on saying all those things you are expected to say and feel you ought to say – in your relationship, your social life or your workplace – if they aren't what you really want to say. What comes to the fore instead, because more energy has become available for it, is the expression of something quite different. At a relatively superficial level, it's just telling people all the things you've thought but never dared say, and enjoying seeing how shocked they all are (even though, of course, they knew all along really, but were just keeping up the pretence too). There are lots of films on this theme; *American Beauty* is the most recent and one of the best. They are about a fortyish man who starts to tell the truth to his boss or to his family or to the electorate, and the audience loves it.

But at a deeper level, there is something really important going on. You are not just telling the truth to others, you are telling it to yourself as well. For a few people, the truth is that you've chosen a way of life that is just right for you, makes the best use of your abilities and will bring you all you want from life; for these unusual people the mid-life crisis slips by almost unnoticed. For the rest of us, for whom the message is a good deal less palatable, it is a huge challenge. It is a clarion call to change. Accordingly many men and women make enormous life changes at this kind of age, and largely for good reason; they are letting go of all the ways of being which they adopted when younger not because they were right for them but because they were the best strategies they could devise for dealing with all kinds of external pressures and inner unconscious motivations. It is disruptive, of course; but in a way that's the whole point.

There is another aspect to this as well. Looking at yourself afresh at this age, and telling yourself the truth, the chances are you'll see all sorts of things you don't much like. In the language of psychology, you are seeing your shadow; a composite of all the unrealized and unacknowledged aspects of yourself. In the language of this book, the energy of the fifth chakra wasn't sufficiently activated to bring them to light. Whichever language you use, suddenly you are aware of these hidden potentials. Everybody has them, but it is alarming when you first realize that you have in you all the qualities you most dislike in others. And you probably also notice minor ways in which you have acted out these qualities, and hurt others as a result. A part of beginning to tell yourself the truth about who you really are is admitting that you aren't as squeaky clean as you thought.

This is the briefest of descriptions of what is happening in a mid-life crisis, but it is enough to make it obvious that the person who is going through this change might unwittingly start to undermine the relationship. For one thing, the focus on him or herself will take attention away from being part of a couple, and that aspect of life may become a little thin and undernourished. More powerfully, it may seem that the relationship binds him into a set of expectations and demands which are keeping him trapped into who he was and won't let him be who he now is. To be sure, this is an overdramatic way of putting it, but people can get a bit overdramatic at this time. They say things like 'I can't go on living a lie', and 'I have to sing my song' and get very upset if you find the exaggeration comic. The relationship may also suffer when one or both partners start to notice the less agreeable aspects of themselves which they've managed to ignore before. If he starts to see meanness, cruelty, indifference in himself, then the chances are he'll be more aware of them in her too – after all they are there in all of us. In fact, rather than look too closely at these aspects of himself, there is a danger that he might jump to the conclusion that they are far more hers than his, and start to question why he is with her.

It can be a really difficult time, but there is plenty you can do to get through it. Stay at interface as often as you can, so you don't spiral into mutual reactivity with your partner. Try and keep your heart protector open by doing things you love, especially with him or her. To keep the energy moving so it doesn't go toxic, take up Yoga or Chi Gung or Tai Chi, or take a course of energy medicine treatments. It would be tempting to believe that what you have to do is to renegotiate many of the agreements and understandings you have with your partner; probably some of them will now seem inappropriate or outdated. But the danger is that this will weaken the container of your energies just when it needs to be strong. It would be better to remind yourself of what they are, maybe even talk to your partner about them and see if you can come up with an agreed version. Instead of thinking this is the ideal time to change them, it is really the time to stick to them meticulously.

There is a communication technique which can help too.[4] At these times, it is easy either to disappear into your own thoughts, or to embark on long and elaborate rationalizations of who you are and what you're doing, neither of which will foster genuine communication. To start the technique, get into the habit of noticing any feeling that arises when your partner says or does something. I don't mean any thought; it has to be a sensation you feel in your body – for example, a flutter in the upper chest, a weakness in the legs, a pain in the back or a loss of air in your chest. I don't even mean noticing an emotion. To think 'I feel angry', for example, is to have taken one step away from the sensation itself. Say instead something like, 'I feel red in the face and as if I'm about to burst.' If you then go on, 'I have an urge to throw something' that's pretty close to reporting a sensation; but better would be, 'I feel as if my arm wants to pull back and then whip forwards.' The closer you can get to the immediate physical sensation the better. The next step is to report this feeling to your partner. Don't analyse it, explain it or justify it. Simply report what you feel. There are a number of reasons this technique can be helpful at difficult times. For one thing, it stops you jumping to conclusions which fit in with what you think is going on, interpreting your reactions before you really know what they are. Hence you may find that, actually, you don't mind something you thought annoyed you, or you do feel open to a suggestion you assumed you'd reject. Then you can communicate that to your partner rather than the well-worn position you've adopted. For another, it avoids the seductive temptation of justifying yourself, which usually entails making your partner wrong. It has a neutral quality to it. Finally, it can open up a really good conversation because it is often more interesting than the customary grievances or complaints. Your partner may be intrigued, for example, that you feel as if your legs are empty. She may suddenly understand why, when she gets angry, you just stay immobile in your chair; previously, she took that as a sign of indifference. She may realize how her body responds to stress, and talk to you about that. This kind of conversation may not seem very fascinating, but it is about something which your partner didn't know and it is about something real and true.

If you try this technique and find it helpful, you can adapt and extend it. A good variation is to notice small ways in which you attack or undermine the relationship, and then report these to your partner. You might say, 'I know you don't like it when I stay up watching TV when you go to bed. Usually

I do it when there's a programme I really want to watch, but last night there was nothing special on. I just felt lazy and couldn't be bothered to move.' You might get a huffy response, but to some degree it will change the energy between you, and the more you do it the more it will change.

So much for the downside of the mid-life crisis; there is an upside too. The fruits of the inward focus can be rich. Giving so much time and attention to work, children and all of that, it is easy to lose touch with yourself, rather as you might lose touch with an old childhood companion. Meeting him or her again, someone who knows you without all the trappings of your adult life, and falling back into familiar ways of being can be very comforting and nourishing. Letting go of some of who you are supposed to be and allowing out some of who you actually are is an enormous relief and can be a doorway into a way of life that feels more genuine and authentic. And there is an opportunity to relate to your partner from this deeper place too, to meet each other more nakedly and more equally in the knowledge that you have each seen, and can love, something essential in the other.

staying still

I have just chosen a few examples of times of change in a relationship; there are plenty more I haven't discussed, like the birth of a first child, retirement, moving house and so on. You can work out how to apply the principles I've mentioned to these too, although you may have to modify the detail a bit as you do so. But there is one more idea which is relevant to all times of change. It is to practise staying still.

What I mean by this is allowing some time each day when you stop being busy with all the things you have to do, stop trying to work things out, and stop chasing your thoughts. It is so much harder to recognize, understand and appreciate what is going on around you if you are constantly doing something. If, on a walk through a wood in the evening, you hear a sound which you can't quite place, you instinctively stop. It is easier to locate and identify the sound when you are still than when you are moving. It's the same if you get a quick glimpse of something; you freeze in order to see it better. At times of change what is happening is similarly unfamiliar, and you can't be sure what it is or what it means unless you stop to take notice.

The other reason is that the very act of stopping has a powerful energetic effect. In the midst of change your energy will be a bit chaotic and you'll feel a lot better and be able to cope more skilfully if it gets more organized. The single best thing you can do to achieve that is to stop. Energy sorts itself out, becomes more coherent and better balanced, if it has a still point around which to organize. For example, a normal handshake doesn't have much effect on your energy, especially if it is accompanied by conventional words – that's one of the reasons it's the normal way of greeting strangers. But holding someone's hand absolutely still, especially in silence, makes quite an impact. You wouldn't welcome this from a stranger because it would affect your energy body. If you watch world-class golfers or snooker players, they prepare and rehearse the shot they are about to play a number of times. Then, when they are ready, they address the ball and pause before they make the shot. That's the same thing. The still point around which their energy organizes so it can do exactly what they want it to do. This pause is only for a few seconds, but in relation to the time taken by the shot, it's a significant proportion. If you think of the amount of time you spend thinking about the problems you face at difficult times, or the amount of time you spend rushing about to avoid thinking of them, the equivalent would certainly be more than a few minutes.

It is easy to stop being busy but not nearly so easy to stop thinking, planning, worrying. Find something that helps your mind to get quiet. Usually, that will be something that requires concentration as opposed to thinking. Many meditation techniques are based on concentration so they have this quietening effect, but scraping old paint or swimming may do it just as well for you. Whatever you do, aim to do it for about forty minutes continuously each day – for some reason that period of time works best. The point is to take a break, not so much from your normal activities but from your normal thinking. You'll emerge refreshed and better able to cope; as if you've had a good sleep. As Shakespeare showed so vividly in *A Midsummer Night's Dream*, in that time away from normal life the unconscious mind can sort out all the muddle and confusion so that you wake up with the problem solved and harmony restored.

chapter seven

separation

For all pairs of lovers, without exception, bereavement is a universal and integral part of our experience of love. It follows marriage as normally as marriage follows courtship or as autumn follows summer. It is not a truncation of the process but one of its stages; not the interruption of the dance but the next figure.

C.S. Lewis, *A Grief Observed*[1]

Separation is experienced at two levels simultaneously. There are the immediate feelings which come up when a relationship ends, temporarily or permanently, and there are the deeper memories and echoes of past separations which are evoked again by the current event. The feelings you have when parting from a partner are overlaid and amplified by older ones. Seeing a loved one off at an airport can bring up sensations of loss and abandonment, however sternly you may tell yourself that it is nonsense to feel that way.

All of us have had early experiences of separation and loss, some of them traumatic for a child even if they wouldn't seem so to an adult, and we remember them not just in our minds but in our bodies too. It can be startling for those who have never previously experienced skilled bodywork to find, in a session, that a strong image of a childhood parting, accompanied by strong emotion too, can suddenly come to consciousness. The person receiving this form of treatment may even smell an odour which was present at the time, or hear sounds which were happening in the background. The practitioners won't be surprised; it happens all the time. Touch at a particular place can activate long-forgotten memories, sometimes with great richness of detail. If one were to examine the tissue of the body at the place which was touched, there would be nothing to see; there is no physical trace at the spot. So it seems likely that the memory is held in the energy body. Perhaps the moment of separation came as a great shock and the energy body contracted under its impact. That contraction may still be there, somewhat like a knot in a piece of wood. Touch it in the right way, and what caused it is almost as fresh and as present as in the moment it happened.

As well as evoking the memories of early loss, a separation will have a direct effect on the energy body. Grief, like all emotions, is a particular movement of energy. When people weep with grief they slump, the face goes white, the voice goes weak and has a falling, exhausted quality to it – all indicating that energy is being withdrawn inwards. It is the opposite of the energy of anger; instead of moving up and out, energy goes in and down. At the same time there may be all sorts of other changes in the energy body – separation may also involve shock, betrayal, anxiety, anger and resentment, and all of them will have an effect too.

What happens energetically when a couple separate is a complex combination of the past and the present, the adult and the child, the deeper and the more superficial levels of the energy body, so it is not surprising that separation can hit us so hard and take so long to get over. Although there are many explanations of what is happening to people who are grieving and many methods of helping people come to terms with loss,[2] it is instructive to look at separation as an energetic phenomenon and to see how working with the energy body can help people to recover from it.

In what follows, some of what I say will apply to temporary separations, where one partner is away for a matter of weeks or months – especially if there is anxiety about commitment or sexual fidelity. But the focus is on permanent separation; on when, for whatever reason, the partners stop sharing their lives. Except for those few who marry their childhood sweetheart, stay with him or her and die first, such separation is a part of any intimate relationship.

limbo

The early days of a separation are a kind of limbo. This is felt most strongly by one partner if the other dies or leaves the relationship suddenly. In that case, it is the shock which first pushes a person into this state, and he or she will commonly say, 'I fell to pieces.' That's an accurate report of how it feels because shock scatters energy. It is as if a flock of birds, roosting in a tree, is startled by a gunshot. Until the energy body settles down again after the shock, as it will, the person will find it difficult to concentrate on anything, even the simple tasks of normal existence. Perceptions of the world will be distorted; time will go very quickly for a while and then, for no apparent reason, it will go very slowly. Nothing seems real. All this because the energy body, which is a kind of faculty like thought or speech, isn't functioning normally.

Even if there is no surprise, the early days, weeks and months after separation will leave both of the former partners in at least a mild form of limbo. Essentially, that is because they will tend to be mulling over the past and worrying about the future. It is natural to be filled with memories, regrets and thoughts about where and how it went wrong and what could have been done to prevent it. Particularly acute will be the recollection of those small but apparently pivotal moments, the hug that was not offered, the unreasonably harsh words, the refusal to compromise in some argument, those scenes being replayed with different outcomes. It is also natural to be filled with fears about the future. As well as the perfectly sensible worries about money or children there may be deeper fears about being alone, about being unlovable, about being a failure. In a wild oscillation, thoughts can turn from fears to fantasies, imagining remarkable futures which wouldn't have been possible while in the relationship. Understandable though it all is, the important thing is to recognize that such thoughts are just a symptom of fragmented energy. The symptom itself, like any other symptom, is worth taking seriously as a signal that something needs to be healed. But the content of the thoughts is not worth taking seriously. If we have a physical symptom, like a broken leg or an infection, we regard it dispassionately and take the appropriate action; but because this symptom appears as thoughts we don't view it in that way. We identify with the content of the thoughts and take them as some truth about ourselves. Instead of attending to the content we need to turn our attention to the mechanism.

Going into limbo is a mechanism for avoiding the present, and we do it by scattering our energy to the past and the future. The present is painful, and all our instincts are to avoid pain. Unfortunately, avoiding it prolongs the limbo. The way out of this awful no man's land is to focus on being in the present. It will be an effort because it will be swimming against the tide of our inclination, but that is what is needed to bring our energy back together, and without doing that we can't begin to heal. The way to do it is to concentrate on what is being felt at any one moment.

The basic procedure is the same as has appeared, in different guises, throughout the book. Put attention on your body and let it roam through until something catches your attention. It's a bit like using one of those metal detectors which are waved above the ground and bleep when there is metal below. As soon as you notice something, stop roaming and concentrate on it. Now describe it to yourself as accurately as possible. Avoid reporting in generalities or abstract concepts, such as 'betrayal' or 'grief' or 'abandonment'; they are one step away from the sensation itself. Try to pinpoint it instead. You don't have to do anything with your observation, don't have to judge it as good or bad or try to work out why you are feeling what you're feeling. The point is to help you to come back to the present because that will bring your energy back into one coherent form again. It is one way of breaking a vicious circle.

There is an interesting and important secondary effect of bringing your attention to the sensations in your body. When you are in the grip of a strong emotion, say you're in despair or depressed, it seems as if that is everything and everywhere; there is no part of you separate from the despair or the depression. Nor is there any partner there now to pull you out of it. To repeat the analogy I used in chapter four, there is no one on the river bank to throw you a life line. But if you can report on your body sensations, then there must be some part of you which isn't in despair or depression.[3] The part that is reporting isn't in that state; it is just reporting. That part can be, so to speak, on the river bank throwing a life line. Or, to say the same thing in another way, there is you observing that you are in limbo and depressed in the same way that you might observe that you are out in the rain getting wet or out in the sun getting hot. You aren't the rain or the heat, just as you aren't the depression; they are just affecting you. Like the sun and the rain, the depression is just energy doing its thing. You get wet or hot or listless, but that isn't the whole story. Once you know that, and you can only know it by bringing your attention back to the present again and again, then you start to emerge from the limbo.

disconnecting

When two people are intimate over a long period of time their energy bodies become interdependent. Quite how they do so, and what it feels like, varies from couple to couple; figure 4 gives three examples. In the first example, the two energy bodies are mainly self-contained, but they are open to

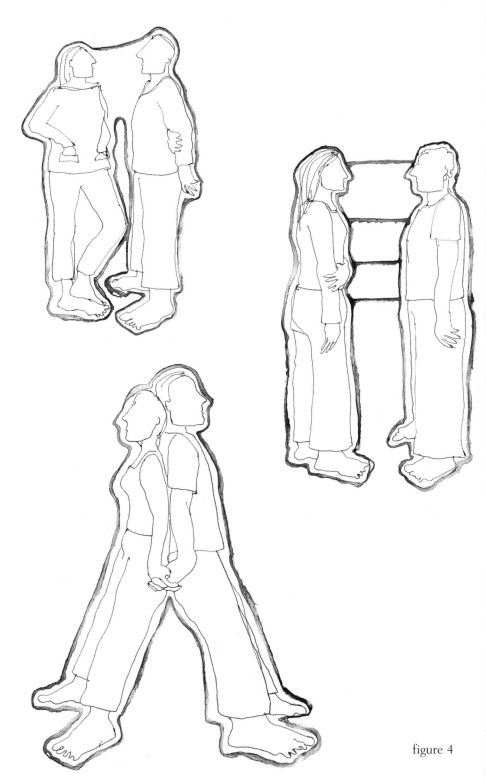

figure 4

each other over quite a large area, and join easily there. When this couple separates, their energy bodies will be weak and unprotected at the place where they used to meet and merge. Consequently these people will feel exposed and vulnerable, and they may well become touchy and hypersensitive as a result (if you are a friend, trying to help, don't be surprised if they take your sympathetic remarks as a personal affront). They may even have the strange feeling that they don't know their own body. When I separated from my partner, my body felt like a coat that didn't belong to me, and one which was threadbare at various places so the wind whistled through.

In the second example, the energy bodies are connected by strands. Although the couple's energy bodies haven't merged they are tied together through having shared times of great elation, difficulty, sadness and so on. When the couple separates, these strands don't break, they just stretch, rather like melted cheese. However far apart they are physically, these strands keep the couple bound together energetically. They will have the strange sensation that, even without direct communication between them, each knows what the other is feeling, even doing, at times of heightened emotion, and they'll often be right. In the last example, the two energy bodies have mutually supported each other, and the withdrawal of that support leaves each feeling unstable, unprotected and unwilling to trust. It is as if each had been leaning on a wall, and the wall has suddenly been taken away. I have distinguished these types of interdependence because there is usually one predominant mode of connection; but in any long-term relationship there will be some element of all three.

Whatever the particular nature of the connection between the two energy bodies, breaking that connection can be very uncomfortable. It can leave each person with an unfamiliar energy body, and if he or she doesn't understand what has happened, it is bound to be alarming. It also involves giving up something to which the energy body was deeply accustomed; it is no exaggeration, I think, to say that it is as difficult for the energy body to do that as it is for the physical body to give up an addiction to a powerful drug. All this is sensed as a feeling of being lesser, incomplete.

So people tend to reach for quick, simple solutions. One is to find a new partner as fast as possible. That works reasonably well for the first and third examples – the hole in the energy body is plugged by connection with another, or there is, once again, another energy body to lean on. It doesn't work so well where the energy bodies of the old couple were predominantly connected by strands; the old ones don't disappear while new ones, with a new partner, are being created. That explains the awkward state people get into when they feel love for a new partner, but can't help feeling closer to the old one, and can't help being deeply concerned with what he or she is doing.

The other quick solution is to keep the old energetic connection going. In other words, what happens is that when the ex-partners meet, they immediately join, or lean, or activate old strands. It is such a relief. Even if it is only for a hour or two, at least it is a break from the discomfort. This is why some couples go through a sequence of separating and getting back together again, often over and over again. The reasons for separating are still there, but so is the energetic connection, and the couple wobble between giving effect first to the one and then to the other. If they want to break out of this oscillating behaviour, they either have to change their minds about the reasons they separated or make a clean disconnection between their energy bodies.

In fact, sooner or later, all couples who separate have to make a clean disconnection of their energy bodies.[4] Otherwise old ways of behaving will be introduced into the new relationship. For the energy body isn't passive – it forms some of the preferences, biases and habits which make us behave the way we do. If your energy body stays connected in some way to a former partner, you might find it hard to learn to enjoy life with a new one. You might find fault unnecessarily and reject delights if they don't fit in with what you are used to. For until the energy body is whole again, the need to heal it is so powerful that it can dominate all intimate or potentially intimate encounters. Needing another to help you heal keeps the focus of your attention on yourself and on a constant checklist of 'Am I getting enough here?' With this focus it is easy for all kinds of manipulation and coercion to creep in, leading you to behave towards the other in ways which will get them to give you what you want. It doesn't work, because even if he or she does give you what you want there's a bit of you that knows that it was a put-up job. You don't really want someone who has to be pushed into meeting your needs; you want someone who loves you. More important, you want someone to love, and with the focus on yourself you won't even notice the other person as a person, let alone love him or her. In the language of chapter five, your energy will be coming only from the lower chakras.

Those who have a period on their own after separation will probably find it easier to make a clean disconnection between the energy bodies. But whatever the circumstances, it will help if you do something conscious and deliberate to restore the individual wholeness of your own energy body. The various forms of energy medicine work well in this respect (see appendix one, page 128). Some people have found visualization techniques useful, too.[5] The outcome of restoring the energy body will be an integrity – both in the sense that it becomes whole again on its own, and in the sense that the person will then be able to relate to others with integrity.

grief

If you think of grief as an emotion, it is strange that we feel it in two very different sets of circumstances. Grieving is perfectly understandable when we have lost something we hold dear, when a loved one has left or died. But we also feel grief when a relationship ends even if we know it was more a source of pain than of pleasure, and even if it is a tremendous relief to be free of the pressures it entailed. In the first case, grief is expected and welcome; sobbing and crying certainly help. In the second case, grief comes as a surprise and it is confusing; how can we grieve for something we no longer want, for something which, often after long and agonizing deliberation, we have chosen to be without? Understanding the energy of grief explains this puzzle and gives some clues about how it can help us to recover from a separation.

Experienced as a movement, grief is a tightening, a squeezing, a contraction. When sobbing with grief, the sobs seem to be forced out from the centre like water being squeezed out of a sponge. Tears flow and mucus comes out of the nose as if expelled by an inner pressure. The body hunches up, the arms come into the chest and the legs up to the stomach, as when the body is trying to empty a constipated bowel. Those who are grieving lose their appetite for food and don't want to take in anything else either – they lose interest in what is happening in the world outside. In other words, the energy is concentrated on clearing out. And that is immensely helpful. So much of what was accumulated in the old relationship – shared ways of living, experiences of intimacy, hopes and plans for the future, an instinctive knowing of each other – no longer has a part to play in our life and needs to be discarded. Letting go of all that isn't easy, and the strong and effortful contraction of grief serves to push it out. And until the old has been discarded there really isn't room for the new to come in. Those who don't grieve properly, who ignore or resist this energetic impulse, miss the opportunity to let go and take much longer to recover fully from a separation. All this is true whether or not the relationship was a happy one and whether or not a person is glad that it has ended. Energy doesn't take much notice of judgments of what we think is right or wrong.

In this description of grief it may seem as if I am muddling up physical, emotional and psychological states; evacuating a constipated bowel is not the same as discarding hopes for the future. But energetically there is no distinction. What moves a person will move their body, their mind and their emotions all together. Although it is often useful to regard the physical and the psychological as different, doing so can obscure the fact that a person is one whole thing and that the distinctions between different aspects of ourselves are in our minds not in the individual human being. As we respond to what life brings, the response will manifest throughout the whole, whether or not we choose to think of it that way.

The energy of grief does more than help us discard the old: it helps to change us too. After a separation we will have to change, whether we like it or not. In the case of the death of a partner this is obviously true, but it applies when a couple split up as well. The partners will need to adjust to living in a new environment, whether it is a physical, emotional or psychological environment or some combination of the three. More important, however much one partner blames the other for the split, and however impossible was his or her behaviour, each of them played a part in the disintegration of the relationship and each has something to learn from it. I realize that this may sound harsh to those who have separated from partners who were violent, abusive, addicted or mentally ill, and in these extreme instances perhaps there is nothing more to say. But far more often there is some way in which both partners created, colluded in, allowed or simply failed to stop a process which unravelled the relationship and demolished what they hoped would be a lasting source of joy. For each of them, it is whatever led them to participate in the way that they did which needs to change.

It is genuinely difficult to change; the way we are in a relationship is not completely malleable. Some of it is an innate disposition. Some of it comes from what we learned as children. Some of it was set in place by adult experiences of living with a partner. All of it hardens into a set of habits, expectations and assumptions.

Where do these
Innate assumptions come from? Not from what
We think truest or most want to do:

Those warp tight-shut, like doors. They're more a style
Our lives bring with them: habit for a while,
Suddenly they harden into all we've got
And how we got it;

Philip Larkin, *from* 'Dockery and Son'[6]

If we enter into the next stage of life without changing, still dancing, puppet-like, to the old tunes, then the chances are that we will find ourselves repeating what we have done before. And it takes something really powerful to crack those assumptions. The energy of grief, allowed to flow freely, has that power.

Think of these hardened assumptions and habits as a piece of metal – a knife, a horseshoe or a wrought-iron railing – which is strong and rigid and has a particular shape which doesn't change in daily use. But apply enough heat and it can be altered dramatically. The heat which melts the metal allows the smith to hammer it into a new shape. By analogy, the intensity of the movement of energy in grief is the fire, and the strength of its contraction are the hammer blows. It is a very uncomfortable experience and a relentless one at the time, but it does forge something new from the old material.

So much for the benefits of grief. As with all energies, it becomes toxic if it gets stuck. If, after an appropriate time for mourning, the inward contracting energy continues, the result can be a set of troublesome physical symptoms and behaviours. There may be problems with breathing and the lungs. The lungs need to expand and fill, and the tightening energy of grief inhibits that natural movement. There may well be problems with the colon too; if grief goes on too long, its energy becomes passive and instead of expelling the old it holds on to it.

Again, the physical and the psychological aren't different; they are both manifestations of an energetic state. So those with lung problems may well become depressed, introverted and reclusive, cut off from other people and lacking the energy it takes to absorb anything new and start on another phase of life. Those who care about them and want to be with them may feel that they are being rejected and abandoned; it isn't that these grieving people don't want to be with their friends, they just haven't the energy it takes to respond to them. Those with colon problems will be like Queen Victoria. After her husband, Prince Albert, died she kept rooms exactly as they were, and even had his clothes laid out for him and his shaving water brought in each day. This is a bizarrely extreme case, but there are plenty of people who are still deeply attached to a loved one who died ten years ago, or to a relationship which ended long in the past. It's not that they remember with affection and gratitude, which is entirely healthy; it's that they haven't got over their loss and constantly fantasize that their life would have been fine if it hadn't happened.

The solution, as always, is to get the energy moving again. After a while, it is best for those who are stuck in grief to avoid people who are in the same state or who insist on being sympathetic; both of these will feed the grief. Allowing oneself to feel any other emotion will help too – given that they are different movements of energy, they will counteract the energy of grief. If it is difficult to access other emotional states, others can help by offering them as a gift. When I was grieving longer than was appropriate, one of my daughters said to me, 'Get a life, Dad!' That is the energy of anger – not angry but forceful. With it in front of me, as a model, I was able to access that energy in myself again.

healing

I started this chapter by saying that the separations we go through as adults evoke the separations we had as children. As children we didn't have the resources to deal with the grief, anxiety and fear that we felt then, and as a result they left their mark on us. If we look deeply at the difficulties we encounter in relationships we can see how the same things seem to happen again and again; unconsciously, and energetically, the way we relate to others is deeply influenced by the mark of our early experiences and the attitude we took to them. For one woman, the penny dropped only after her third marriage ended, like the two previous ones, after fourteen years. She suddenly made the connection with the fact that her father had died when she was fourteen. As a child her attitude to her loss was to say to herself, defensively, 'I don't need you, Dad. I can manage – in fact, I'm better off without you', and this message was stamped, somehow, on to her energy body ready to be reactivated at the appropriate time. As one well-known therapist says, 'Tell me what you fear and I will tell you what has happened to you.'[7]

In normal life we remain blissfully unaware of the mark left by these early experiences. But at a time of separation that isn't possible. We don't have to dig down into the psyche or into the past to find it; it is what is happening, again, and what we're feeling about it, again, and how we are reacting to it, again. But this time, with an adult's resources and awareness, we can notice all that and start to change it. Ironically, the pain and distress of separation provide the necessary conditions for healing.

There are many effective ways to heal; religion and ritual are very old ways, analysis and other forms of therapy are new ones. I want to add to them the way of energy. To a considerable extent, the energetic sensation of loss and the initial energetic response to it will be the same this time as before. That's because the mark left on the energy body by the early separation is being reactivated by the present one. If the energy body can be healed this time, then the healing will inevitably and automatically apply to the past, to all the separations. If the energy body is changed it is changed, and it won't be the same again. And the basic method of changing it is to be fully in the experience of grief and loss; neither to embrace it nor reject it, neither to wallow in it nor deny it, and certainly not to evaluate it. In order to do that, all that is required is to keep on bringing one's awareness to the body's energy in the moment – and not then do anything about it. This sounds absurdly simple, but the healing takes place from allowing the grief to be as it is and living it. It isn't easy – simple doesn't mean easy – but it does change the energy body. And if you think about it, it isn't so surprising that this has such a powerful effect; how seldom do we humans stop trying to avoid pain and give it instead our full and undivided attention?

do it yourself

Romantic love is the single greatest energy system in the Western psyche . . . It is up to us, as individuals, to take this raw unconscious energy of romantic love, this confusing array of impulses and possibilities, and transform it into awareness and relatedness.

Robert A. Johnson, *We: Understanding the Psychology of Romantic Love*[1]

I read the words I have quoted above many years ago and instantly knew that the author was right. But I didn't know, and he didn't really explain, how to transform romantic love into awareness and relatedness. Nor could I see any way of deriving how to do it from the basic idea that we all have this raw unconscious energy. It was only much later, when I became completely convinced that each of us has an energy body and that it works in a consistent and coherent fashion, that I could begin to grasp how seeing love as energy might be a practical proposition.

As I learned more about the energy body from my work as a practitioner of energy medicine, I came to understand that it responds quickly and powerfully to attention. At first I assumed this response could only happen if the practitioner had years of training in the particular theories, concepts and techniques of at least one branch of energy medicine. But the more experienced I became, the more I realized that it was something both simpler and deeper which enabled change. It was simpler because most of what I had been taught as a student boiled down to some pretty basic ideas and a lot of very precise techniques. But if I was working with my own energy, or collaboratively with a partner on the energy of the relationship, the techniques became irrelevant and there wasn't a great deal which had to be learned. It was deeper because so much of it had to do with a quality of presence; of really being with someone and really paying attention to him or her. I suppose that this kind of presence reaches another level – both for the one giving and for the one receiving attention. As the giver, you stop thinking about what you want, what impression you're making, what to say next and so on. In that state you are in touch with something that lies behind or beyond personality – yours or the other person's. I've called it energy. Whatever you call it, and whatever it is, it is real. Relating to another in this way feels peaceful, kindly and safe. As the recipient of this kind of attention, you feel acknowledged, accepted, and free from the pressures which others put on you, and you put on yourself, to be better in some way. It's like taking off a tight shoe at the end of a long day's shopping – such a relief.

At this level, something else happens which is an enormous relief too. Blame becomes irrelevant. I spent years endlessly judging whether what my partner was doing was right or wrong, good or bad, suited me or didn't; it was practically a full-time job. But when I stopped doing that (or, to be honest, occasionally managed to stop doing that) and actually paid attention to her, I began to see how her energy was just doing what it was doing. There was no more point in judging it than I would judge a tree or a thunderstorm. It simply was what it was, and it was behaving as energy behaves. Nor was there any point in taking it personally, because it wasn't aimed at me. Of course there were times when she got angry or critical, or told me things that upset me, and I could take all that personally if I chose to. But I didn't have to. It was her energetic response to what I had said or done as part of the situation she found herself in, that was all. I could just give her my attention, and later I could look at what she was complaining about and decide whether or not to change it.

I suppose the next stage of my learning about all this was when I found that I was being grumpy or resentful or critical. With my new understanding of energy, blame was no longer an option, but on the other hand I couldn't stop having the feelings either; I couldn't turn them off by an act of will. I felt trapped. I'd gone too far to go back, but not far enough to escape out at the other end. What finally got me out of the trap was realizing that I could change my own energy state. I tried it and it worked. The resentment and criticism disappeared. Having shifted my blocked energy I no longer had the same feelings or emotions, no longer went round and round with the same thoughts. What I felt and thought wasn't some immutable truth; it changed as my energy changed.

Then it slowly dawned on me that I could no longer pretend to be a passive observer of my relationships, being tossed around by their ups and downs. Even less could I pretend I was a victim of my partner or of the dynamic we had created. If I could change my own energy, then I had to take responsibility for its state. If I chose not to even attempt to change it, I was choosing to stay angry, dissatisfied, helpless – to keep things as they were. Taking responsibility for my own energy entailed taking responsibility for all the moods, thoughts and behaviours that it stimulated. Of course, I railed against this conclusion. I wanted to go back to the illusion of powerlessness, which felt so much more cosy to me. A childlike state, I suppose. But when I stopped railing, I could see that there were gains too. As a friend wrote to me, 'You sail along thinking you're not doing anything significant, it's all trivial everyday stuff, hardly worth paying attention to. Then Wham, you're off the edge of the world, and you suddenly realize it all mattered, it was all important, every single thing. There is no trivial moment in your entire life. The message: you matter; it all matters. That's quite a gift to find in your hands.'

Then I noticed that when I changed my own energy, the energy of the relationship changed too. In fact, I realized, it couldn't help but change. If you have a system and you change half of it – imagine changing half the components of a car or half the staff of an organization – then the system as a whole will be different and it will behave differently too. In the past, when I wanted to improve the energy between us, I either asked her to change or I tried to take us into complex negotiations about what we each wanted and needed and all that. Hopeless. For one thing you can't change another person – only they can change themselves; for another, the negotiations emphasized our separateness when what we needed was for us to come together. It was worse than hopeless, actually; it was unfair. If I wanted to change the energy of our relationship, it was up to me. I could do it myself simply by changing my own energy. If you want to change the energy of your relationship, do it. It's nice if your partner wants join in, but it isn't necessary. You can do it yourself.

How do you do it? Well, the whole of this book has been about that, but there are a few key ideas. The main one is to stay at interface. In the end, that's largely a way of making sure that you're in a position to pay attention to your partner. If you lose interface, then when you look at your partner it is as if you are looking in a mirror and seeing yourself reflected in him or her. You'll be like Narcissus, who fell in love with his own reflection in the water, loving your own image and not your partner. I'm sure there are lots of ways of avoiding this, but the way to do it with energy is to keep your energy body separate from your partner's. The more you can keep your energies separate, the more intimate you can be. I know that seems like a paradox, but paradoxes are matters of logic and grammar and energy is neither logical nor grammatical.

Another key idea is that you need a container for the energy of your relationship. It's like a bowl for water or a grate for fire. If the energy isn't held in, then it will escape. It may leak away until there's none left or it may set fire to the house and burn it to the ground. In an intimate relationship, the container is a complicated set of mutual understandings about what expectations are legitimate, about boundaries which are not to be broken, and limits to the energy that each partner can take beyond those boundaries and use in the outside world. The limits can be about very simple things, like not telling others intimate details of the relationship or about spending time off work together. They can be about more complex things, like loyalty to your partner in the face of pressures from parents or siblings, about how close you can be with potential lovers. Each couple will make different choices about where the boundaries lie, but they need boundaries and they need to rebuild them consciously and deliberately if they are broken.

The fact that stuck energy becomes toxic is fundamental too. Like blood, energy needs to circulate. If you fall asleep lying on your leg in such a way that the blood supply is cut off and then try to stand up, your leg won't work. And it is agony when the blood starts to flow into it again. It is very much the same with energy, though the timescale is much longer. Fearful of change, a couple may try to keep the energy between them predictable and stable instead of encouraging it to move at the first signs of discomfort. If they do, the chances are that they will be generating exactly what it is they are trying to avoid. Hold on to a solution for too long and however good it was when it was fresh it will eventually go mouldy.

Being stuck is not the same as being still. If your energies get out of balance, if one partner's demands, needs and expectations seem to be dominating the relationship, remember that energy will rebalance around a still point. So have times together where you are still, not doing anything much and not talking much either. John Bayley and Iris Murdoch had a long and very happy marriage, and their love seems not to have been affected by the Alzheimer's disease which overwhelmed her in her last years. He said, '[Our marriage] was one of those curious kinds of closeness where we never bothered each other at all. We just had a sense of being together . . . we were like two animals in a field.'[2] This is especially important if you sense that the imbalance between your two energy bodies may be setting up a vicious circle, as one energy feeds on the other. A time of stillness helps you to become aware of what's happening and that will at least stop the momentum of the spiral, and give you the breathing space to work out what to do to break it.

Don't forget to give your heart a chance. Given only half a chance it will lead you to feel love and kindness towards your partner and enable a deep level of communication between you both. It will help you to forget about all those petty irritations which can be so depressing and disempowering for you both. The heart will illuminate the best in him or her, so you can both see it more clearly and appreciate it more fully. If you feel your heart protector closing when you are alone together, do something to open it again so you can get back to intimacy. Your brain will probably say that this is romantic nonsense, and instruct you severely to listen only to its messages of distancing and caution. It's reasonable to take note, but it is irrational to live only from your brain. In the end it cuts you off from what you are bound to discover you hold most dear.

Finally, I said in chapter one that the book was about what an intimate relationship might be like when you don't depend on your partner to be in love and perhaps you can now see what I was getting at. The 'raw unconscious energy of romantic love' is what kick starts the process of getting your energy to amplify the love, affection and intimacy you feel for your partner. From then on it's up to you. You know that you have the power to keep it going or to stop it and put it in reverse. If you choose to keep it going, you don't need your partner to be anything or do anything in order to be in love with him or her. You're just in love and he or she is included. It's contagious, of course; your partner will get it and you'll get it back again, and so on.

It is easy to sleepwalk through life and relationships, to let it all drift by. But energy is happening in the moment in every moment, and in each moment it gives the potential to change things for the better. To take full advantage of it in the moment isn't to be thoughtless or careless about the future. On the contrary. In Thich Nhat Hanh's wonderful words, 'The best way to look after the future is to take good care of the present.'[3]

energy medicine

All forms of medicine have an effect on the energy body, but many of them take no account of it and may leave it depleted or disorganized. Some forms of medicine, in general known as complementary medicine, are either designed specifically to enhance the energy body or reliably have that effect. This appendix gives a brief introduction to these forms of medicine and the way in which they can help a relationship.

The ones I know fall into two basic categories. One category comprises those which work explicitly with energy; for instance Acupuncture, Homeopathy, Shiatsu, Zero Balancing, Aromatherapy, Colour Therapy, Reiki and some kinds of herbal medicine. In another category come those therapies which undoubtedly benefit the energy body, although that is not their rationale or focus; here I am thinking of McTimony Chiropractic, Craniosacral Therapy, Rolfing and Feldenkrais. There are plenty more complementary therapies, and some of them might fit into these categories; I haven't included them here because I don't know enough about them. I have excluded massage and osteopathy because although there are practitioners of both who undoubtedly work effectively with the energy body, my experience is that, in general, these forms of treatment do not reliably help it.

Generalizing, I think it is fair to say that the forms of medicine in the first category are based on quite detailed and specific knowledge of how the energy body works, and practitioners will plan what they do to have specific effects on it. To what extent they are successful is, of course, another matter. For those in the second category, change in the energy body comes more as a beneficial side effect; the treatment is aimed at something else, and improvement there helps the energy body. In other words, the work done is entirely compatible with the anatomy and physiology of the energy body.

The basic proposition of this book is that the nature of an intimate relationship is partly the outcome of the state of the energy bodies of the partners. If the partners are finding it difficult to relate to each other easily and joyfully, some of that can be attributed to a dissonance between their energy bodies; their relationship will improve if their energy bodies become more harmonious. There are many possible causes of dissonance, and the choice of a form of treatment depends, to some extent, on the cause. If one partner has been suffering from stress for a long time, is weary and run-down, and has an energy body which is both depleted and disorganized, then any form of treatment will help that person and hence the relationship. If the problem is more specific, then it may be more appropriate to use a treatment that works explicitly with energy. For example, if one partner has had a very specific shock – felt betrayed by a close colleague, felt responsible for some accident or injury to a child, has felt obliged to lie to protect someone – then there is likely to be a specific and localized injury to the energy body. In this case, it might be preferable to choose a form of medicine from the first category.

Having said that, personal preference is more important than any apparently objective criteria of choice. If you like and trust the practitioner, the treatment will do far more good than if you don't have confidence in what he does, or if you get irritated by his manner or behaviour. As I have said many times in the book, energy responds to attention; so if you feel you aren't getting his full attention, then however good and appropriate the treatment may be in theory, it won't evoke much response in you. In addition, take seriously your preferences about the form of treatment itself. If you can't bear the thought of needles, don't have Acupuncture. If you really like to be touched, then choose one of the forms which uses it; and if you like touch but don't like getting undressed before a stranger, choose Zero Balancing rather than massage. It isn't hard to collect basic information about the methods used by each form of treatment; you can ask friends about the treatments they've had, and most practitioners have leaflets which describe what they do.

As I have suggested throughout the book, the energy of the relationship will normally and automatically respond to a change in the energy body of one partner. However, if the energy bodies of both partners need help, it will speed up the process if they both have treatment. Normally, it doesn't matter if they choose different forms of treatment – any is better than none. However, if both partners are happy with the same form, and indeed the same practitioner, I think the effect is amplified. Speaking as a patient, I have found that when my partner and I had treatment in this way it often had the effect of re-establishing intimacy between us.

Speaking as a practitioner, I have found it very satisfying to treat couples. I can't explain fully what difference it makes, but what happens is, roughly, as follows. Treating the first partner, I gain a knowledge of the state of his or her energy body and also see how it has changed through the course of that session. When the next partner comes in, I instinctively compare the state of that energy body with his or her partner's. I get some impression of the gap that there was between them, and of the gap that now exists, given that one has been treated and the other has not. All that information gives me a sense of direction for the treatment, a more specific and precise idea of what would help. Perhaps all it amounts to is that I can be aware that I am treating a couple as well as an individual.

To put flesh on the bones, so to speak, I finish with a story. It illustrates many of the ideas in this appendix, and indeed in the book as a whole. However, as with any true story, it doesn't do so neatly and precisely; but I choose to stick to the truth rather than tidy it up.

The client was a woman in her mid-forties. She suffered from sexual abuse when a child. In the past ten years or so she had done a huge amount of work around this issue, which had been successful in that she was much more comfortable in her body than before, was happily married and no longer suffered from depression.

However she had one remaining symptom which caused her great difficulty. As part of her work as a therapist she attended a group in which the participants recounted some story or issue in their lives, and it was important that they do so as truthfully as possible. The anticipation of having to tell the story of her abuse, as well as the less frequent experience of actually telling it, evoked enormous anxiety in her. It took her a long time to recover peace of mind afterwards, and until she did she felt distant from her partner. Indeed, her attendance at the group was becoming a serious bone of contention between them. She regarded it as essential to her work; he thought it was threatening their marriage.

She had come for a Zero Balancing session to deal with this issue in some way. We agreed that if she felt this anxiety during the session, she would pay the closest possible attention to it and describe it, to herself silently or out loud, in the most accurate possible detail. In that way we hoped to find its true nature, extent and power. If a memory of the abuse was evoked she would report on that; if not, she wouldn't link what she was feeling, by habit, with the memory of her experience.

The first time she felt anxiety was when I was working on her left foot. To her surprise, she felt the anxiety in her jaw, at the top. She observed it closely. It made her jaw feel stiff and achy, but it did not spread and it did not bring up memories of abuse. It lasted perhaps twenty seconds and then faded. She was interested and pleased that this was the only effect. With her permission I repeated exactly what I had done before on the left foot, although this time I amplified what I was doing a little. Again, she felt anxiety immediately. This time, as well as in the same place in the jaw it was also in her left lumbar area. She was disappointed and worried. 'It's getting bigger,' she said. 'Just observe,' I replied. It faded from both areas within about ten seconds. Again, with her permission, I repeated the work on her left foot. This time, the anxiety was in her jaw again. It was very mild and lasted only a few seconds.

She opened her eyes and looked at me. 'Is that it, then?' she asked. Then she answered her own question. 'What I actually felt was a few seconds of anxiety in my jaw. Nothing else.' She went on, 'If I'm in a workshop and I'm feeling anxiety in my jaw, then that is what I report; I don't have to say anything about the abuse. In fact, it's more than that. It isn't really telling the truth if I go into the abuse – that isn't, in fact, what is coming up.'

Since then she has often felt anxiety in the group, but it hasn't lasted more than a few seconds, and she has no difficulty being close to her partner when she gets home.

omissions

Throughout this book I deliberately chose not to distinguish between the energy of a man and the energy of a woman. This may seem eccentric or simply wrong. I think it is worth explaining why I wrote the book in this way.

Much has been written about the different biology of men and women and how this affects personality, attitudes and assumptions; the vagina as compared to the penis, male and female orgasm, testosterone as against oestrogen, hunters and homemakers, and so on. I don't know how true this all is, nor how much of it is intrinsic or is the result of centuries of socialization. However it is clear that groups which are all male behave very differently from those which are all female, that generally women have a stronger instinct for nurturing babies than men, and that the vast majority of violent crimes are committed by men. In addition, from my own clinical experience, I have felt differences between male and female energy.

In spite of all this, the key question is whether we learn more about relationships through emphasizing the differences between men and women or by stressing the similarities. There are times when emphasizing differences is useful. The energy of a woman changes dramatically during pregnancy, especially in the later stages. Her physical body is so involved, moment by moment, with sustaining the new life which is growing within her that her energy is pulled in towards the centre to encircle the womb. At that time, the energy of her partner is not physically affected in this way; if it changes at all, it will be in the opposite direction in order to deal with the demands of the outside world. But in most circumstances, certainly in relation to the topics I have chosen to discuss, I think it is unnecessary and unhelpful to distinguish between men and women. I don't believe, personally, that a man's love or anger or sense of grief is different from a woman's. Equally, the nature of the chakras is the same for both, and the blending or interface touch used by a man or a woman is the same.

Another notable omission is that the book does not refer to the distinction, much used in energy medicine, between two contrasting qualities of energy known as Yin and Yang. The energy of daytime, for example, is considered as Yang; it is active, busy and outgoing. The energy of night-time, on the other hand, is quiet, withdrawn, passive: that's Yin. They are two aspects of the energy of a single day. One is not better and the other worse; both kinds of energy are essential parts of the whole. It is the same whatever whole you take – whether it is a cell of the body, which has both a negative and a positive electrical charge, a human being which has to have periods of activity and periods of rest, or a year with the contrasting energies of summer and winter, autumn and spring.

The manifold ways in which these two kinds of energy combine and change provides a powerful and sophisticated way of understanding energetic change. It forms the basis of the *I Ching*, probably the oldest known book, which is a manual of decision making, an aid to divination and an analysis of the way change happens. Certainly, the energy of relationships can be seen as an interaction of Yin and Yang. For example, it can provide an explanation for the fact that opposites tend to attract. If one person has an energy body which is mainly Yin, quiet and receptive, he or she will be attracted to a person whose energy body is mainly Yang, active and forceful, and vice versa. They will instinctively recognize that they are two halves of a whole. This is a theme played out endlessly in stories and fantasies. The film *Notting Hill*, for example, is the story of a quiet and rather ineffectual man, that is a person who is predominantly Yin, winning the love of a beautiful international film star, who is predominantly Yang. Hence, the story goes, behind her powerful façade the woman is Yin at heart; *The Taming of the Shrew* is based on this idea too. It also suggests that a man who is predominantly Yin can beat all the more Yang men who have always made him feel inadequate and win the prize of the most desired woman in the world. This has enormous appeal to all those men, the overwhelming majority, who can't see themselves as Yang heroes.

After much deliberation two reasons persuaded me to leave out this way of looking at the energy of a relationship. One is that it leads easily to a facile correspondence that men's energy is Yang and women's is Yin. This is, in my view, to misunderstand both the true meaning of these concepts and the true nature of energy in human beings. It also seems to entail an emphasis on the differences between the energy of men and that of women which, for reasons I have explained, I found unhelpful. The only way I felt I could overcome this problem was to write a long and detailed explanation of how

Yin and Yang are seen to operate; and that would have overwhelmed the book.

Also with some regret, I omitted any reference to astrology. Much modern astrology is based on the notion that each planet has a particular energetic quality; and the position of each planet (or 'placement', to use the technical term) at any given time brings out a particular aspect of that energy. For example, the planet Uranus has a quality of revolutionary change which is often sudden and unpredictable. Its placement will also suggest aspects of life – for example, work or relationships or health – in which that change is likely to appear. The placement will also suggest the time at which the impetus for such change will be strong. The whole topic of looking at intimate relationships in this way has been covered in a book called *Relating* by Liz Greene (see the bibliography on page 136). I chose not to refer to this perspective on relationships simply because I'm not an astrologer, and felt that I didn't have sufficient depth of knowledge to write about it accurately.

Finally, and for the same reasons, I also decided to omit much reference to psychological concepts. Many of these are powerful and illuminating and can be of enormous help in explaining what happens in intimate relationships. In addition, while writing, I was often struck how many of these concepts parallel the energetic concepts I have used to reach the same kinds of conclusions. I am sure that an investigation of the relationship between the energy body and the psyche would open up a whole new level of understanding; but it was beyond my abilities and the scope of this book.

••• bibliography

Books about relationships which I have enjoyed and which have helped me (in no particular order).

The Art of Loving
Erich Fromm, Harper & Row, New York 1956.
A short and elegantly written book which gets below the surface of the idea of love and talks about the principles of being loving.

Relating: An Astrological Guide to Living with Others
Liz Greene, Aquarian, London 1977.
A truly original book and a classic. Full of wisdom, psychological insight and wry humour.

Soul Mates: Honouring the Mysteries of Love and Relationships
Thomas Moore, HarperPerennial, New York 1994.
A wonderful combination of the spiritual, the psychological and the magical, seeing the value of our confusions and apparent mistakes in relationships.

We: Understanding the Psychology of Romantic Love
Robert A. Johnson, HarperSanFrancisco, New York 1983.
Based around the story of Tristan and Iseult, this is a clear, concise explanation of the psychology of love.

Teachings on Love
Thich Nhat Hanh, Parallax Press, Berkeley 1998.
Written by the Vietnamese monk, scholar and poet, this is a Buddhist perspective of love and relationships.

Getting the Love You Want: A Guide for Couples
Harville Hendrix, HarperPerennial, New York 1990.
A clear and convincing account of some basic psychological ideas about relationships; simple but not trivialized. Has a good set of exercises for couples.

Conscious Loving: The Journey to Co-Commitment
Gay Hendricks and Kathlyn Hendricks, Bantam Books, New York 1992.
A very similar book to the one above.

Nature, Man and Woman
Alan Watts, Vintage Books, New York 1991.
An iconoclastic book, using deep understanding of Daoist thought to illuminate issues in relationships.

And a large number of tapes by Ram Dass, for example 'Getting Free Together', available from Living Dharma Tapes, Poulstone Court, Kings Caple, Herefordshire, HR1 4UA, tel. 01423 840860 and The Hanuman Foundation Tape Library, 524, San Anselmo Avenue, No 203, San Anselmo, CA 94960, tel. 1-800-248-1008.

••• notes

page 10 The extract is from an untitled poem. See *Selected Poems 1923–58*, e.e. cummings, Faber and Faber, London 1960, p. 29.

introduction

1. *A Life of One's Own*, Marion Milner, Virago, London 1986, p. 178.

2. The 'impossible questions' about fists and laps come from *The Way of Zen*, Alan Watts, Penguin, London 1990, pp. 75–6.

3. *Valerie V. Hunt, Infinite Mind*, Malibu Publishing Co, California 1989.

4. The image of two pieces of wood joined by a dowel comes from a talk by Thich Nhat Hanh.

5. *Iron John: A Book about Men*, Robert Bly, Addison Wesley, New York 1980.

6. The village blacksmith mentioned here is in *Akenfield*, Ronald Blythe, Penguin, London 1999.

7. I owe the distinction between attention and intention to Dr Fritz Smith.

8. *The Quantum Self*, Danah Zohar, Flamingo, London 1991, pp. 26 and 28.

9. *Plant Spirit Medicine*, Eliot Cowan, Swan Raven, Oregon 1995, p. 52.

chapter one

1. *Soul Mates*, Thomas Moore, HarperPerennial, New York 1994, p. 151–2.

2. *Energy Medicine: The Scientific Basis*, James L. Oschman, Churchill Livingstone, London 2000, p. 121.

3. The idea of being in a state of love comes from Ram Dass. He talks about it on many tapes – I first heard it on one called 'Who Turned Right?', which is also the source of the quotation from Mother Teresa.

chapter two

1. From a talk given by Thich Nhat Hanh in July 1995 at Plum Village, France.

2. *Middlemarch*, George Eliot, Penguin Classics, London 1994, p. 425.

3. The concepts of interface and blending come from Dr Fritz Smith. As his interest is mainly in therapeutic touch, I have adapted his ideas to this context, with, I hope, as little distortion as possible.

4. From 'The Thieves'. See *Selected Poems*, Robert Graves, Penguin, London 1986.

chapter three

1. *The Hero's Journey*, Joseph Campbell, ed. Phil Cousineau, HarperSanFrancisco 1990, p. 159.

2. For a fuller account of emotions as energy see *The Seven Emotions: Psychology and Health in Ancient China*, Claude Larre and Elisabeth de la Vallee, Monkey Press, Cambridge 1996.

3. I haven't been able to find the source of the notion attributed to Thomas Merton.

4. *A Life of One's Own, op. cit.,* pp. 106–7.

5. For much fuller information about the energy of the heart see *The Heart's Code: Tapping the Wisdom and Power of Our Heart Energy*, Paul Pearsall, Broadway Books, New York 1999.

6. *The Quantum Self, op. cit.,* p. 119.

7. *Plant Spirit Medicine, op. cit.,* p. 52.

chapter four

1. *Journey to Ladakh*, Andrew Harvey, Picador, London 1983, p. 195.

2. For much more on the heart protector see *Dragon Rises, Red Bird Flies – Psychology and Chinese Medicine*, Leon Hammer, Station Hill Press, New York 1990.

3. The idea of refusing to have the next thought comes from Gangaji. See, for example, *You are That: Satsang with Gangaji* Volumes 1 & 2, Satsang Press, Boulder, Colorado 1996.

4. Some people claim that, with skilled guidance, the practice of hitting pillows transforms the energy of anger. Judging by my own experience, and from what I know about how energy works, I cannot agree.

5. The notion of a container has many sources. I found it first in Jung's accounts of alchemy, and have also drawn on the teaching of Dr Fritz Smith in a workshop entitled 'The Alchemy of Touch'.

6. *Anna Karenina*, Leo Tolstoy, Chapter 23, Part 2.

7. *Emmanuel's Book II*, compiled by Pat Rodegast and Judith Stanton, Bantam Books, New York 1989, p. 63.

chapter five

1. *Enchanted Love: The Mystical Power of Intimate Relationships*, Marianne Williamson, Rider, London 1999, pp. 86–7.

2. *Molecules of Emotion*, Candace Pert, Scribner, New York 1997, p. 245.

3. For a fuller, and somewhat different, description of the chakras see *Anatomy of the Spirit*, Caroline Myss, Bantam, London 1996.

4. I have not been able to find a reference for Joseph Campbell's analogy of light and light bulbs.

5. The line 'I'll love you if you pretend I am who I think I am (and in return I'll pretend you are who you think you are)' is from Ram Dass. He uses it on a tape called 'The Yoga of Relationship'.

chapter six

1. *The Hero's Journey, op. cit.,* p. 63.

2. *This Business of the Gods*, Windrose Films, Ontario 1988, p. 16.

3. The idea of a torch comes from Ram Dass. He uses it on many of his tapes.

4. There are many variants of the communication technique I describe. I have drawn most on one in *Conscious Loving: the Journey to Co-*

Commitment (see bibliography, p. 136) where it is called 'telling the microscopic truth'.

chapter seven

1. *A Grief Observed,* C.S. Lewis, Faber and Faber, London 1976, pp. 42–4.

2. On Bereavement I have drawn on the work of Elisabeth Kubler-Ross, especially *On Death and Dying,* Tavistock Publications, London 1970.

3. The idea that there is a part of you that is not grieving comes from Ram Dass.

4. The basic idea of a 'clean disconnect' is Dr Fritz Smith's.

5. For visualization techniques see *Cutting the Ties that Bind,* Phyllis Krystal, Sawbridge Enterprises, London 1982.

6. From 'Dockery and Son'. See *The Whitsun Weddings,* Philip Larkin, Faber and Faber, London 1964.

7. From an article by Adam Phillips in *The Guardian Weekend,* 14 February 1998, p. 34.

conclusion

1. *We: Understanding the Psychology of Romantic Love,* Robert A. Johnson, HarperSanFrancisco, 1983, pp. xi and 4–5.

2. From an article in *The Guardian* (2), 31 August 1999, p. 5.

3. This quotation from Thich Nhat Hanh appears on postcards published by the Community of Interbeing, Plum Village, France.

publishers' acknowledgments

The publishers are grateful to all the copyright holders mentioned above who have given permission to reproduce work in this book. All reasonable effort has been made to trace copyright owners of quoted material, but the publishers would be happy to rectify any errors or omissions in future editions of the book.